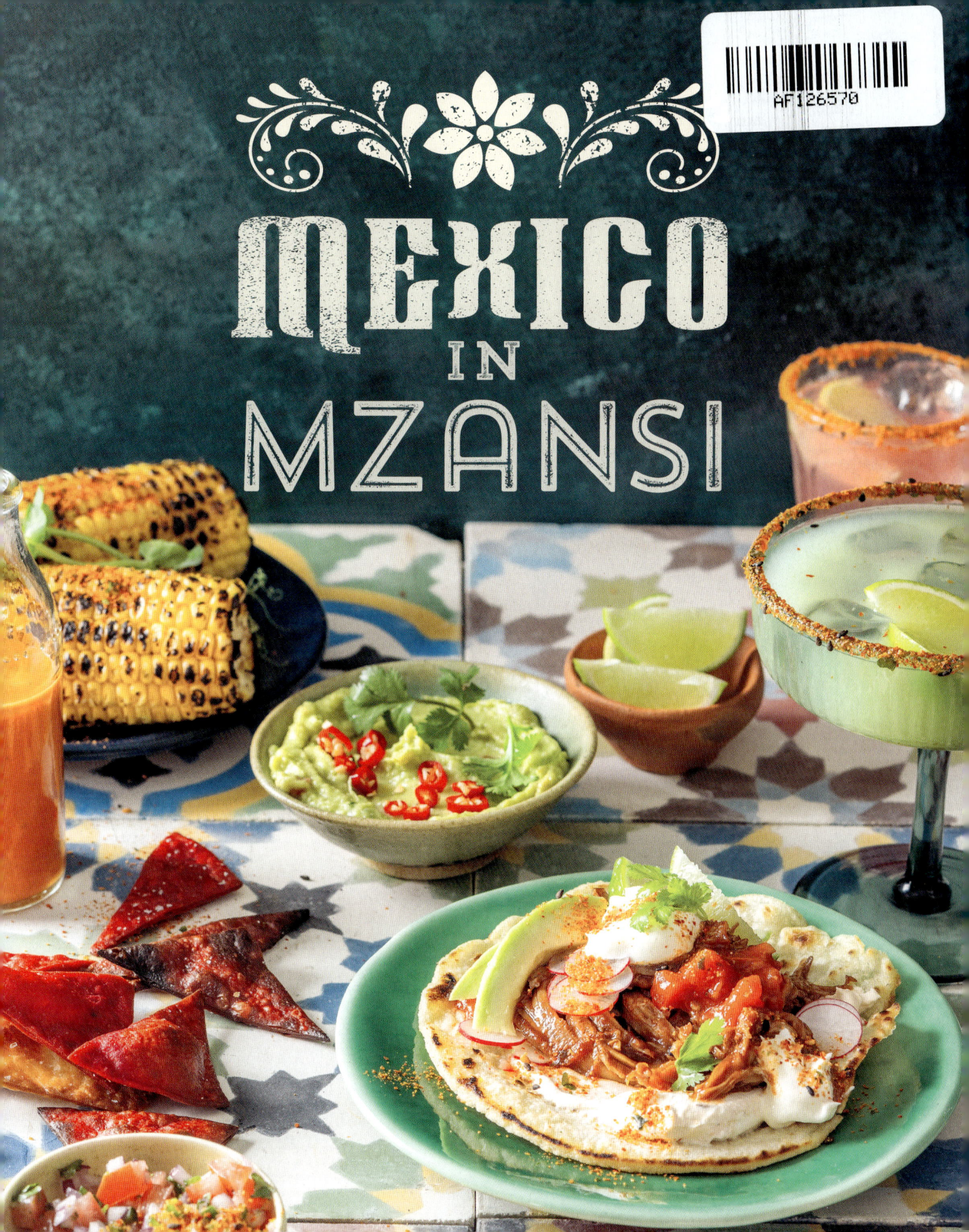

PUBLISHED IN 2024 BY PENGUIN BOOKS,
an imprint of Penguin Random House South Africa (Pty) Ltd
Company Reg. No. 1953/000441/07
The Estuaries, 4 Oxbow Crescent, Century Avenue, Century City, 7441
PO Box 1144, Cape Town, 8000, South Africa
www.penguinrandomhouse.co.za

Copyright © in published edition:
Penguin Random House South Africa (Pty) Ltd 2024
Copyright © in text: Aiden Pienaar 2024
Copyright © in photographs: Penguin Random House South Africa (Pty) Ltd 2024

ISBN 978-1-48590-182-2

All rights reserved. No part of this publication may be reproduced, stored in a retrieval system or transmitted, in any form or by any means, electronic, mechanical, photocopying, recording or otherwise, without the prior written permission of the publishers and the copyright holders.

PUBLISHER: Beverley Dodd
MANAGING EDITOR: Aimee Sinclair
EDITOR: Bronwen Maynier
DESIGNER: Randall Watson
PROOFREADER: Anita van Zyl
PHOTOGRAPHER: Donna Lewis
STYLIST: Caro Gardner
ASSISTANTS: Elizma Voigt; Ellah Maepa
INDEXER: Cecilia Barfield

Reproduction: Studio Repro

Printed and bound in China by
Golden Prosperity Printing & Packaging (Heyuan) Co., Ltd.

CONTENTS

Introduction 6

Basics 9

Tacos 32

Quesadillas and Enchiladas .. 54

Tapas 74

Mexico Meets Air Fryer 102

Desserts 118

Margarita and Co. 132

Recipe Index 154

INTRODUCTION

It all started at the tender age of ten, when my parents would host these elaborate Mexican-themed parties for their family and friends. It was a spectacle. Fajitas, margaritas, tequila, guacamole, freshly cut limes, you name it, it made an appearance on that dinner table. I was fascinated by the aromas that filled the house, not to mention the flavours. I was hooked!

Some years later, I opened my first Mexican restaurant in Port Elizabeth, South Africa. Nestled in the heart of the city, it was a small, thirty-four-seater, with a kitchen no bigger than a food truck. While the concept and flavours centred on Mexican cuisine, it was by no means an authentically Mexican restaurant. While I served many traditional and well-loved Mexican classics, I also took inspiration from all corners of the globe, especially my home country, Mzansi.

This book is no different. Yes, you will find authentic Mexican dishes, but, like the ubiquitous taco, it is filled with a surprising array of flavours and influences from all over the world. I love researching and experimenting with new ideas and flavour combinations to excite even the most experienced chefs. While some of these recipes can take minutes to prepare, others may take hours, but one thing is certain, the result is worth it.

All the recipes are easy to follow and those suitable for vegetarians are marked with a (V). Just remember the golden rule, whether you're cooking a meat dish or a vegetarian one: always keep it FRESH.

Now sit back, relax and enjoy a little bit of Mexico in Mzansi ...

BASICS

These are the essential components that you will need for many of the dishes in this book. They are all multifunctional and not exclusive to the recipes in this book, so make them yours and incorporate them into your everyday cooking!

TIP
I recommend using the tortillas on the same day you make them, but they can be kept in an airtight container in the fridge for up to 2 days. Do not freeze.

CORN TORTILLAS

Masa harina (a gluten-free maize meal) is widely used in Mexico and South America to make tortillas. Once you master the technique of making the perfect tortilla, the world is your oyster, so to speak.

MAKES 55 TORTILLAS

2kg masa harina
4 tsp salt
6–8 cups warm water

1 Combine the masa harina and salt in a large mixing bowl. Stirring continuously with a wooden spoon, gradually add enough warm water until a dough begins to form. Then, using your hands, knead the dough for 2 minutes in the mixing bowl, shaping it into a smooth ball. The dough should feel springy and firm, like playdough. If it feels too wet and is sticking to your hands, add a few extra tablespoons of masa harina. If it feels too dry and crackly, add in an extra tablespoon or two of warm water.

2 Weigh out the dough into 30g balls. Place each ball between two pieces of clingfilm in the centre of a tortilla press and, in one swift motion, press the top part down to flatten the dough. Alternatively, roll out each ball of dough with a rolling pin to 2–3mm thick and 12cm in diameter.

3 Heat a non-stick pan over medium heat. Once the pan is nice and hot, peel away the clingfilm and place the tortilla gently into the dry pan. Cook for about 40 seconds on each side, or until small brown spots or speckles begin to appear. The tortilla should puff up slightly.

4 Once the tortilla is cooked, place it on a plate and cover with a clean tea towel to keep it warm while you cook the remainder.

PICO DE GALLO
(FRESH TOMATO SALSA)

MAKES 3–4 CUPS

1 red onion, diced
8 Roma tomatoes, deseeded and diced
2 jalapeño chillies, deseeded and finely chopped
⅓ cup chopped fresh coriander
juice of 2 limes
pinch of salt
4 tsp canola oil

1 Combine the red onion, tomatoes, jalapeño chillies and coriander in a bowl.

2 Add the lime juice, salt and oil and give it a good stir. Taste and adjust the flavours, adding more salt or chilli if needed.

> **VARIATION: ROASTED CORN SALSA**
> Grill a corn cob on an open fire to get it nice and charred, then cut off the kernels. Braaiing the corn will give the salsa an extra smoky flavour. Add the charred corn kernels to the bowl along with the rest of the ingredients.

TIP
Remember, you can always add, but never take away, so rather add a little than a lot when adjusting for taste.

BASICS

PICKLED RED ONIONS

MAKES 6 CUPS

1L water
½ cup white wine vinegar
4 tsp white sugar
1 tsp salt
8 red onions, finely sliced

1. Bring the water, vinegar, sugar and salt to a rolling boil in a small pot.
2. Add the sliced red onions and allow to boil for 10 seconds, then remove the pot from the heat and pour the contents into a metal bowl.
3. Leave to cool before transferring to an airtight glass jar.
4. Store in the fridge for up to 3 months.

VARIATION: PICKLED RED CHILLIES
Replace the red onions with 400g whole red chillies.

TIP
Try not to use your fingers to remove the pickle from the jar, as the oils in your skin can turn the pickling liquid rancid and reduce shelf life.

BASICS

CHIPOTLE CHILLI MARINADE

This marinade makes a great addition to stews and soups. You can also use it as a basting, or turn it into a delicious dipping sauce – just add 500g sour cream at the end.

MAKES **1 CUP**

200g chipotle chillies in adobo sauce

2 tsp ground cumin

1 tsp chopped garlic

1 tsp cayenne pepper

¼ cup lemon juice

2 tsp paprika

½ tsp salt

1 Place all the ingredients into a food processor or blender and blend until smooth.

2 Store in the fridge in an airtight container for up to 6 months.

Lime and Coriander Marinade

MAKES 2 CUPS

¼ cup lemon juice
40ml canola oil
¼ cup ground cumin
2 Tbsp cayenne pepper
1½ cups chopped fresh coriander
pinch of salt

1. Place all the ingredients into a food processor or blender and blend until smooth and emulsified.

2. Store in the fridge in an airtight container for up to 2 days.

TIP

The oil might separate as it sits in the fridge – just give it a good shake before using.

GUACAMOLE

MAKES 10 CUPS

8 ripe avocados

1 red onion, finely diced

4 tomatoes, deseeded and chopped

1 jalapeño chilli, finely diced

55ml lime juice

⅓ cup chopped fresh coriander

1 tsp ground black pepper

2 tsp salt

1 Scoop the avocado flesh into a large bowl and mash with a fork.

2 Add the rest of the ingredients and give it a good mix.

3 Taste and adjust for seasoning – you are looking for a balance between salt and sour with a pop of freshness and crunch from the onion and tomato.

REFRIED BLACK BEANS

I love beans! Any kind of beans. This recipe became an instant favourite.

MAKES 1½ CUPS

½ cup olive oil
1 small white onion, chopped
4 cloves garlic, crushed
1 tsp ground cumin
1 tsp chilli powder
4 x 400g can black beans in brine
salt and ground black pepper to taste
½ cup chopped fresh coriander
¼ cup butter

1 Heat the olive oil in a small pot over medium heat. Add the onion, garlic, cumin and chilli powder and cook for 5 minutes until the onion turns translucent.

2 Add the can of black beans with their brine, season with a pinch each of salt and black pepper and stir to combine. Leave to simmer for 10 minutes or until most of the liquid has evaporated.

3 Turn down the heat to low, add the coriander and butter and stir vigorously to break up the beans. Check for seasoning. It should have a 'fall off the spoon' consistency.

4 Store in the fridge in an airtight container for up to 3 days.

TIP
Reheat the beans with a small amount of butter and water.

BASICS

MOLE NEGRO

Mole is a rich Mexican sauce made from chillies. Mole negro, or black mole, is the smoothest of the moles and has the most depth of flavour. Mole can be served with most things, from tacos and enchiladas to roast chicken. No Mexican cookbook would be complete without a mole recipe.

MAKES 16 CUPS

- 24 dried ancho chilies, deseeded
- 2L warm chicken or vegetable stock
- 2 cups seedless dark raisins
- olive oil for frying
- 2 large onions, chopped
- 12–15 cloves garlic, crushed
- 4 tsp chilli powder
- 4 tsp ground cumin
- 4 tsp ground coriander
- 2 tsp ground cinnamon
- 1 tsp ground nutmeg
- 1 tsp ground cloves
- 2 tsp dried origanum
- 1½ tsp salt
- ¼ cup chipotle chilli marinade (page 16)
- ½ cup tahini (sesame paste)
- ⅔ cup chopped bitter or semi-sweet dark chocolate

1 Toast the ancho chillies in a dry pan, then add them to a blender along with the warm stock and raisins. Set aside to allow the chillies to soften.

2 Heat a touch of olive oil in a cast-iron pan over medium heat, then fry the onion and garlic until soft. Add the chilli powder, ground spices, origanum and salt and warm through slightly to release their aroma.

3 Add the onion mixture to the blender with the chillies and stock. (You can do this in two or three batches if needed.) Blend until smooth and then pour the sauce straight back into the pan. Cook for 10 minutes over medium heat.

4 When the sauce turns a rich, dark brown, add the chipotle chilli marinade, tahini and chocolate. Stir gently, allowing the chocolate to melt into the sauce. If you feel it's too thick, add a little extra stock. Give it a taste and adjust according to preference: if you want more heat, add more chilli paste; if you feel it needs more sweetness, add some more chocolate.

5 Store in the fridge in an airtight container for a maximum of 4 days.

BEEF SPICE RUB

This spice rub was inspired by my two years working in Dubai. The Middle East really taught me how to use spices in the right way, to get maximum benefit from them. While there are a lot of different spices in this rub, it is totally worth it. You can premix the rub without the olive oil and store it in an airtight container for up to a month.

MAKES ½ CUP

- 2 Tbsp brown sugar
- 2 tsp ground cumin
- 2 tsp ground ginger
- 2 tsp salt
- ½ Tbsp ground black pepper
- 1 tsp ground cinnamon
- 1 tsp coriander seeds
- 1 tsp cayenne pepper
- 1 tsp ground allspice
- ½ tsp ground cloves
- 2 Tbsp olive oil

1. Mix the sugar and spices with the olive oil in a small bowl.

SPICY SESAME MARINADE

MAKES 1/3 CUP

1 Tbsp chopped garlic
2 tsp sesame oil
2 tsp chilli powder
1 tsp ground cumin
2 Tbsp canola oil
½ tsp ground black pepper
1 Tbsp white wine vinegar

1 Mix all the ingredients in a bowl until well combined.

2 Store in the fridge in an airtight container for up to a week.

LAMB MARINADE

MAKES ¾ CUP

1 Tbsp minced garlic
¼ cup harissa paste
1 tsp ground cumin
1 Tbsp brown sugar
¼ tsp ground cinnamon
1 tsp salt
1 tsp ground black pepper
2 Tbsp olive oil
1 tsp smoked paprika
½ tsp ground coriander seeds

1 Combine all the ingredients in a bowl.

2 Store in the fridge in an airtight container for up to 2 weeks.

MEXICAN-STYLE DURKY SAUCE

What could be more South African than Spur's famous Durky Sauce? Here I've put a Mexican spin on the classic buffalo wing sauce.

MAKES 6 CUPS

- 440g chipotle chillies in adobo sauce
- 1 cup lemon juice
- 800ml freshly squeezed orange juice
- 200ml white wine vinegar
- 8 tsp ground cumin
- 4 tsp ground black pepper
- 2 tsp dried origanum

1 Using a stick blender, blend the chipotle chillies in adobo sauce to form a paste.

2 Heat a heavy-based pot over medium heat and add the chilli paste along with the rest of the ingredients.

3 Cook until the sauce starts to thicken slightly, then remove from the heat and allow to cool.

4 Store in the fridge in an airtight container for up to a week.

GARLIC MAYO

You will find this recipe forms the base of many of the sauces in this cookbook.

MAKES 4 CUPS

12 egg yolks
1 Tbsp Dijon mustard
4 cloves garlic
4 tsp salt
800ml canola oil
¼ cup white wine vinegar
lime juice to taste

1. Place the egg yolks, mustard, garlic and salt into a food processor and blitz until smooth.

2. With the blender running, slowly drip in the canola oil until the mixture starts to thicken and emulsify into a mayonnaise. At this point you can pour in the oil in a thin stream.

3. Add half the vinegar and taste (you may not need the rest). Season with more salt and a little lime juice if needed. The mayonnaise should be smooth and thick and slightly tangy.

4. Store in the fridge in an airtight container for up to 3 weeks.

PICKLED CHILLI MAYO

MAKES 4 CUPS

3 cups garlic mayo (above)
24 whole pickled red chillies (page 15)
salt to taste

1. Place the mayo and pickled chillies into a blender and blend until smooth and well combined.

2. Add some pickling liquid to thin out the mayo if needed – this will also act as a seasoning, adding a bit of acidity. Taste and add a pinch of salt if needed.

3. Store in the fridge in an airtight container for up to 3 weeks.

SMOKY CHIPOTLE MAYO

Chipotle chillies in adobo sauce are already very well spiced and seasoned, so you rarely need to add extra seasoning.

MAKES 4 CUPS

3 cups garlic mayo (page 28)

12 whole chipotle chillies in adobo sauce

1 Place the mayo and chipotle chillies into a blender and blend until smooth and well combined.

2 Store in the fridge in an airtight container for up to 2 weeks.

MEXICAN CHAKALAKA

You can't have Mexico in Mzansi without at least one fun twist on the famous South African chakalaka. Instead of navy or kidney beans, we will use black beans and a sprinkle of fresh coriander to elevate the flavours. There's no doubt it's chakalaka, but with a smoky Mexican twist.

MAKES 4 CUPS

olive oil for frying
4 large white onions, chopped
4 cloves garlic, chopped
2 green bell peppers, deseeded and diced
½ cup curry powder
4 tsp chilli powder
4 tsp chipotle chilli marinade (page 16)
10 carrots, peeled and grated
4 x 410g can chopped and peeled tomatoes
salt and ground black pepper to taste
4 x 400g can black beans, drained
½ cup chopped fresh coriander

1 Heat some olive oil in a heavy-based pot over medium heat.

2 Fry the onion, garlic and green pepper until the onion turns translucent.

3 Add the curry powder, chilli powder and chipotle chilli marinade and cook for 1 minute.

4 Next, add the grated carrots and cook for a further 2 minutes, then stir in the chopped tomatoes and season with salt and black pepper. Cover with a lid and cook for about 5 minutes.

5 Add the black beans and cook, covered, for a further 10 minutes.

6 Remove from the heat and stir in the coriander.

7 This can be served hot or cold. Store in the fridge in an airtight container for up to 3 days.

TACOS

The corn tortilla is the most widely used 'vessel' for food in Mexico and some parts of Central America. It's traditionally made from ground hominy (dried corn kernels that have been treated with an alkali), water and salt, flattened into a small disc and cooked on a very hot surface.

Packed with a delicious filling, the humble tortilla is elevated to the venerable taco, which, for me, is the pinnacle of Mexican cuisine. In this chapter, you will find more traditional soft-shell tacos along with others whose roots lie in South Africa, Asia, Spain, Greece and even the Middle East.

CHICKEN TACOS

MAKES 3 TACOS

4 deboned chicken thighs, skin on

½ cup lime and coriander marinade (page 17)

2 baby leeks

sunflower oil for frying

3 warm corn tortillas (page 11)

smoky chipotle mayo (page 29)

1. Marinate the chicken thighs in the lime and coriander marinade for about 5 minutes.

2. In a heavy-based pan over medium heat, dry-fry the marinated chicken thighs, skin-side down, for 10–12 minutes, then flip them over to cook the other side. Keep basting the thighs until browned and cooked through. Remove the thighs from the pan and allow them to rest and cool before cutting them into bite-size chunks.

3. Slice the leeks lengthways as thinly as possible. Heat some sunflower oil in a small pot over low heat to 150°C and fry the leeks until crispy, then drain on paper towel.

4. Fill each taco by spooning some of the chicken along the centre of the tortilla. Place small dollops of smoky chipotle mayo on the chicken and top with some crispy leeks.

TIP Using chicken thighs as opposed to chicken breasts will give you a more flavourful and succulent taco.

CRISPY ASIAN-STYLE CHICKEN TACOS

This recipe was inspired by my trips to Thailand. I remember the distinct mix of sweet and salty; and the spicy peanut sauce that you can quite literally put on anything. The soy sauce will make the chicken very dark in colour – this is to be expected.

MAKES **6 TACOS**

1L canola oil
¼ cup cornflour
½ tsp salt
¼ tsp ground black pepper
4 skinless deboned chicken thighs, quartered
6 warm corn tortillas (page 11)
fresh coriander for garnishing

ASIAN CHICKEN MARINADE

1 Tbsp soy sauce
1 tsp sriracha sauce
1 tsp chilli flakes
1 tsp sesame oil
1½ Tbsp chopped fresh coriander
1 thumb-size piece ginger, minced
2 cloves garlic, minced
½ tsp honey
½ Tbsp rice wine vinegar

PEANUT SAUCE

½ cup unsweetened peanut butter
5 tsp hoisin sauce
¾ tsp chilli flakes
water as needed

ASIAN MEXICAN SLAW

1 carrot, peeled and thinly sliced
½ red bell pepper, deseeded and thinly sliced
½ jalapeño chilli, thinly sliced
1 spring onion, thinly sliced
4 fresh mint leaves, roughly chopped
1⅓ Tbsp roughly chopped fresh coriander
½ tsp lemon juice
pinch of salt

Continues overleaf ⟶

Continued

1 Place the canola oil into a deep-fryer or pot and heat to 180°C.

2 Combine all the ingredients for the Asian chicken marinade in a bowl and mix well. Set aside a small amount of marinade for coating at the end.

3 In a separate bowl, mix the cornflour, salt and black pepper.

4 Coat the chicken pieces in the seasoned flour, shake off any excess and put them straight into the deep-fryer or pot for 30 seconds. Remove them from the oil, dip them in the Asian chicken marinade, then coat them in the seasoned flour once more before returning them to the fryer or pot for a further 40 seconds, until extremely crispy. Drain the chicken pieces on paper towel and then coat them lightly in the marinade you previously set aside.

5 To make the peanut sauce, place all the ingredients into a food processor and blend until well combined and smooth. The mixture will be quite thick, so add a little water at a time to loosen it – you are looking for a honey-like consistency.

6 To make the Asian Mexican slaw, place all the vegetables and herbs in a bowl and mix gently with a spoon until equally dispersed. Add the lemon juice and salt just seconds before serving.

7 Fill each taco by spooning some of the Asian Mexican slaw along the centre of the tortilla. Top with the chicken and small dollops of peanut sauce. Garnish with fresh coriander.

TIP
Serve the chicken tacos immediately to enjoy the delicious crispiness.

CRISPY FISH TACOS

MAKES 3 TACOS

1L canola oil
110g hake fillet
1 tsp salt, plus extra for seasoning
½ tsp ground black pepper
1 cup cake flour
1 Tbsp garlic powder
1 Tbsp paprika
1½ cups sparkling water
¼ cup cake flour seasoned with ½ tsp salt
60g green cabbage, thinly sliced
⅓ cup pico de gallo (page 14)
3 warm corn tortillas (page 11)
fresh coriander for garnishing

PICKLED JALAPEÑO AND CORIANDER SOUR CREAM

¾ cup sour cream
⅓ cup chopped fresh coriander
10g pickled jalapeño chillies
½ tsp salt

1 Place the canola oil into a deep-fryer or pot and heat to 180°C.

2 Cut the hake fillet into manageable, fish finger–size pieces and season lightly with salt.

3 In a large bowl, whisk 1 tsp salt with the black pepper, cake flour, garlic powder and paprika until well combined. While mixing, slowly pour in the sparkling water and keep mixing until you end up with a smooth, lump-free batter. It should resemble a thick crêpe batter.

4 Dip the fish fingers into the seasoned flour, then into the batter. Allow any excess batter to drip off and then gently place the fish into the hot oil. Fry until golden brown and crispy, then drain the fish on paper towel and sprinkle with salt.

5 Place all the ingredients for the pickled jalapeño and coriander sour cream into a blender or food processor and blend until smooth.

6 Mix the sliced cabbage into the pico de gallo and dress it with some of the pickled jalapeño and coriander sour cream.

7 Fill each taco by spooning some of the cabbage salsa along the centre of the tortilla. Add dollops of pickled jalapeño and coriander sour cream and top with one crispy fish finger. Garnish with fresh coriander.

Prawn and Corn Tacos

MAKES 3 TACOS

6 medium tiger prawns

½ tsp cayenne pepper

½ tsp paprika

salt to taste

3 Tbsp canola oil

½ cup Mexican-style durky sauce (page 26)

2 baby leeks

sunflower oil for frying

3 warm corn tortillas (page 11)

⅓ cup roasted corn salsa (page 14)

CORN AND MISO CREAM

2 cups whole corn kernels

¼ cup butter

1¼ cups cream

1 tsp miso paste

1 First make the corn and miso cream. Cook the corn kernels in a saucepan with the butter over medium heat for about 2 minutes. Add the cream and continue to cook for 10–15 minutes or until the kernels are very tender and soft and most of the cream has been absorbed.

2 Remove from the heat and pour the mixture into a blender. Add the miso paste and blend until smooth. The cream will thicken slightly as it cools.

3 Clean, devein and butterfly the prawns, leaving their heads on. Toss the prawns in a bowl with the cayenne pepper, paprika and salt to taste.

4 Heat the canola oil in a large frying pan over medium to high heat. When the oil starts to shimmer, add the prawns and cook until the flesh turns white and slightly pink. Turn them over, they will curl, and cook until the entire prawn turns pink.

5 Add the Mexican-style durky sauce to the pan and make sure the prawns are well coated before removing from the heat.

6 Slice the leeks lengthways as thinly as possible. Heat some sunflower oil in a small pot over low heat to 150°C and fry the leeks until crispy, then drain on paper towel.

7 Fill each taco by spooning some corn and miso cream along the centre of the tortilla. Top with two prawns and garnish with roasted corn salsa and crispy leeks.

BEEF BRISKET TACOS

MAKES 12 TACOS

canola oil for frying

2kg whole beef brisket, bone in

salt and ground black pepper to taste

½ cup beef spice rub (page 23)

12 warm corn tortillas (page 11)

1 pickled jalapeño chilli, sliced into rings

fresh coriander for garnishing

lime wedges for garnishing

HARISSA SOUR CREAM

1 cup sour cream

2 tsp harissa paste

salt to taste

1 Preheat the oven to 190°C.

2 On the stovetop, heat a little canola oil in a heavy-based ovenproof pot over medium heat.

3 Season the beef brisket with salt and black pepper and place it into the pot. Brown it on all sides until a deep golden colour, then remove the beef from the pot and rub it all over with the spice rub. Return the beef to the pot and add some water to cover about a quarter of the brisket.

4 Put on the lid and place the pot in the oven for 2.5–3 hours, checking the water level every 30 minutes. Top up with a little more water if needed. The beef brisket is cooked when you can pull out the bone and it comes out clean.

5 To make the harissa sour cream, whisk the sour cream and harissa paste in a bowl until well combined and smooth. Season with salt as needed.

6 When cooked, transfer the beef brisket to a tray to cool slightly.

7 Return the pot to the stovetop over medium heat and reduce the liquid until thick. While the sauce reduces, shred the beef into a bowl. When thickened, strain the sauce through a sieve into the bowl with the shredded beef. Mix gently and check for seasoning.

8 Fill each taco by spooning some harissa sour cream along the centre of the tortilla. Top with shredded beef and garnish with rings of pickled jalapeño chilli, fresh coriander and lime wedges.

PULLED PORK TACOS

TIP
Colour is flavour, so try to get as much colour onto the pork shoulder as possible.

*An open flame is the best way to colour any type of meat.
It achieves a beautifully smoky, charred flavour that will elevate your tacos.*

MAKES **12 TACOS**

canola oil for frying

2kg whole pork shoulder, bone in

salt and ground black pepper to taste

100g spicy sesame marinade (page 24)

12 warm corn tortillas (page 11)

garlic mayo (page 28)

fresh coriander for garnishing

lime wedges for garnishing

CASHEW AND CORIANDER PESTO

⅓ cup cashew nuts, roasted and roughly chopped

3 Tbsp roughly chopped fresh coriander

1 tsp lemon juice

zest of 1 lemon

2 Tbsp canola oil

pinch each of salt and ground black pepper

1 Preheat the oven to 190°C. On the stovetop, heat a little canola oil in a heavy-based ovenproof pot over medium heat.

2 Season the pork shoulder with salt and black pepper and place it into the pot. Brown it on all sides until a deep golden colour, then remove the pork from the pot and rub it all over with the spicy sesame marinade. Return the pork to the pot and add some water to cover about a quarter of the shoulder.

3 Put on the lid and place the pot in the oven for 2.5–3 hours, checking the water level every 30 minutes. Top up with a little more water if needed. The pork shoulder is cooked when you can pull out the bone and it comes out clean.

4 To make the cashew and coriander pesto, combine all the ingredients in a bowl and mix well. Alternatively, put everything into a blender. Both methods work, depending on how chunky you like your pesto.

5 When cooked, transfer the pork shoulder to a tray to cool slightly.

6 Return the pot to the stovetop over medium heat and reduce the liquid until thick. While the sauce reduces, shred the pork into a bowl. When thickened, strain the sauce through a sieve into the bowl with the pulled pork. Mix gently and check for seasoning.

7 Fill each taco by placing dollops of garlic mayo and cashew and coriander pesto along the centre of the tortilla. Top with pulled pork and garnish with fresh coriander and lime wedges.

BRAISED LAMB TACOS

*Tomato and basil. Fish and chips. Macaroni and cheese.
All classic food pairings, but none beats the greatest of them all: lamb and mint.
Throw in some fresh cucumber and you have a dish that will impress
even the biggest food critic in your family.*

MAKES **12–15 TACOS**

canola oil for frying

3kg lamb shoulder, bone in

salt and ground black pepper to taste

¾ cup lamb marinade (page 25)

4 large red onions, quartered

12–15 warm corn tortillas (page 11)

½ cucumber

fresh coriander for garnishing

pickled red onions for garnishing (page 15)

MINTED SOUR CREAM

¾ cup sour cream

¼ cup fresh mint leaves

juice of ½ lemon

1 Preheat the oven to 190°C.

2 On the stovetop, heat a little canola oil in a heavy-based ovenproof pot over medium heat.

3 Season the lamb shoulder with salt and black pepper and place it into the pot. Brown it on all sides until a deep golden colour, then remove the lamb from the pot and rub it all over with the lamb marinade. Return the lamb to the pot and add the red onions and enough water to cover about a quarter of the shoulder.

4 Put on the lid and place the pot in the oven for 2.5–3 hours, checking the water level every 30 minutes. Top up with a little more water if needed. The lamb shoulder is cooked when you can pull out the bone and it comes out clean.

5 To make the minted sour cream, place all the ingredients into a blender and blend until smooth.

6 When cooked, transfer the lamb shoulder to a tray to cool slightly.

7 Return the pot to the stovetop over medium heat and reduce the liquid until thick. While the sauce reduces, shred the lamb into a bowl. When thickened, strain the sauce through a sieve into the bowl with the shredded lamb. Mix gently and check for seasoning.

8 Fill each taco by spooning some minted sour cream along the centre of the tortilla and topping with lamb. Using a potato peeler, create cucumber ribbons to place around and over the lamb. Garnish with fresh coriander and pickled red onions.

'ROASTED' CAULIFLOWER TACOS

This recipe was inspired by the famous Spanish romesco sauce, which is typically eaten with fish. I wanted to do something a little different, so I worked around my variation of the classic sauce, which is an unusual way of cooking, but we don't judge here.

MAKES 6 TACOS

sunflower oil for frying
½ small head cauliflower, cut into florets
salt to taste
60g green cabbage, thinly sliced
⅔ cup pico de gallo (page 14)
juice of ½ lime
6 warm corn tortillas (page 11)
fresh coriander for garnishing

ROMESCO-STYLE SAUCE

1 whole tomato
½ Tbsp honey
1 tsp chopped garlic
1 tsp ground cumin
2 whole chipotle chillies in adobo sauce
50ml canola oil
½ tsp ground black pepper
1 tsp smoked paprika
1 tsp salt
1½ Tbsp lemon juice
⅓ cup cashew nuts, roasted

1 First make the romesco-style sauce. Over an open flame, char the tomato until the skin is blistered and blackened. Place the tomato with the rest of the ingredients into a blender and blend until smooth. Keep refrigerated.

2 Heat a little sunflower oil in a heavy-based pot to 180°C, then fry the cauliflower florets until golden brown. Drain on paper towel and season with salt.

3 Mix the cabbage, pico de gallo and lime juice in a bowl.

4 Fill each taco by placing some of the cabbage salsa along the centre of the tortilla. Top with cauliflower and dollops of romesco sauce. Garnish with fresh coriander.

TIP

Do not deep-fry the cauliflower for too long, as it will turn too dark and bitter.

SPICY BEEF FILLET TACOS

This taco was born in the comfort of my own home, using what I had in my fridge and pantry. Seasoning this, marinating that, this spicy yet smoky beef taco was the result. It has been a crowd favourite ever since. If you plan to serve the salsa at a later stage, add the lemon juice and salt just before serving.

MAKES **3 TACOS**

100g beef fillet, cubed

2 Tbsp chipotle chilli marinade (page 16)

¼ white onion, thinly sliced

1 Tbsp chopped fresh coriander

2 tsp smoked paprika

1 tsp ground cumin

1 tsp chilli flakes

salt and ground black pepper to taste

4 dashes Worcestershire sauce

3 Tbsp canola oil

3 warm corn tortillas (page 11)

¼ cup plain Greek yoghurt

fresh coriander for garnishing

CUCUMBER AND TOMATO SALSA

⅓ cup deseeded and diced cucumber

¼ cup deseeded and diced tomato

1 Tbsp chopped fresh coriander

2 tsp lemon juice

½ tsp salt

1 Place the beef cubes into a bowl.

2 In a small bowl, combine the chipotle chilli marinade, onion, coriander, spices and Worcestershire sauce, pour over the beef and mix until the meat is well coated.

3 Heat the canola oil in a large frying pan over medium to high heat. When the oil starts to shimmer, add the beef mixture, spreading it out to form a single layer. Once the beef starts to brown, give it a stir and cook to preference.

4 To make the cucumber and tomato salsa, combine all the ingredients in a bowl and mix well.

5 Fill each taco by placing some of the beef mixture along the centre of the tortilla. Dollop on some Greek yoghurt and top with a few spoons of cucumber and tomato salsa. Garnish with fresh coriander.

SOSATIE AND BOERIE TACOS

Having a business in a suburban area, the air was constantly filled with the smell of braai, and this inspired me to create this taco for the iconic and much celebrated Heritage Day in South Africa.

MAKES 6 TACOS

100g boerewors (of your choice)

100g BBQ marinated chicken sosaties (of your choice)

6 warm corn tortillas (page 11)

garlic mayo (page 28)

fresh coriander for garnishing

PAP SQUARES

2½ cups water or chicken stock

1 tsp salt

½ cup maize meal, plus extra for dusting

sunflower oil for frying

1 Make the pap squares. Bring the water or stock to the boil in a large pot over high heat. Add the salt and allow to dissolve. Gradually add the maize meal, stirring continuously. It will thicken dramatically as it cooks.

2 When it begins to boil, lower the heat to medium and cook, stirring continuously, until thick. Reduce the heat further. After 5–10 minutes, the pap will start to come away from the sides of the pot. This is a sign it's ready.

3 Pour the pap into a 29cm square dish to around 1cm thick. Cover with a kitchen cloth and leave for 15–20 minutes until cool and set. Once the pap has set into a solid block, turn it out of the dish and cut into 1cm squares.

5 Heat a little sunflower oil in a heavy-based pot to 180°C.

6 While the oil is heating, toss the cooked pap squares in some maize meal to coat. Shake off any excess and fry until crispy and golden.

7 Start by lighting the braai, if you haven't already. When the coals are ready for some meat action, cook the sosaties and boerewors until juicy and succulent. Allow to cool slightly, then cut into smaller-than-bite-size pieces and mix together in a bowl.

8 Fill each taco shell by spooning some garlic mayo along the length of the tortilla. Top with the meat mixture and crispy pap squares and garnish with fresh coriander.

TIPS

You can make the pap squares in advance. They will keep for up to a week in the fridge in an airtight container. For an authentic South African experience, serve with lashings of Mexican chakalaka (page 31).

QUESADILLAS AND ENCHILADAS

A quesadilla consists mainly of cheese folded in a corn or flour tortilla and cooked in a hot pan. Protein, vegetables and spices are added for extra flavour and nutrition. Quesadillas are best enjoyed with sour cream and guacamole (page 18).

The Spanish word *enchilada* means 'to season with chilli'. An enchilada consists of a corn tortilla rolled around a filling, smothered in a tomato-and-chilli-based sauce, covered with cheese and baked in a hot oven. Enchiladas can be filled with anything from meat and cheese to beans and potatoes. They can be served as a single meal or as a shared dinner with a few added accompaniments such as Mexican-style rice (page 77) and refried black beans (page 19).

QUESADILLA FILLING

This recipe forms the base for the quesadillas in this book.

MAKES 1 SERVING

2 Tbsp canola oil
20g red bell pepper, deseeded and sliced
20g white onion, sliced
1 tsp salt
¼ tsp ground cumin
¾ tsp chilli flakes
¼ tsp cayenne pepper

1 Heat the canola oil in a large frying pan over medium to high heat.

2 When the oil starts to smoke, add the bell pepper and onion and cook for about 1 minute. They should start colouring almost straightaway. This is a good thing as it adds a beautiful smoky flavour.

3 Next, add the remaining ingredients and cook for a further 30 seconds. Remove from the heat and allow to cool.

TIP
Do not add the spices too early, or they will scorch and burn and turn the whole dish bitter.

SMOKED PORK SAUSAGE QUESADILLA

This recipe will work just as well with traditional South African boerewors. The hash-type filling is also great to eat on its own.

SERVES 1

- 1 medium potato, peeled and diced
- canola oil for frying
- 1 large smoked pork sausage, diced
- 1 tsp salt
- 1 tsp smoked paprika
- 1½ Tbsp chopped fresh coriander
- 1 x store-bought 25cm flour tortilla
- ¼ cup grated cheddar cheese
- ¼ cup grated mozzarella cheese

1 Boil the diced potato in a pot of water until firm but fork tender. Strain and allow to cool.

2 Heat a little canola oil in a frying pan. When the oil starts to shimmer, add the potatoes and fry until golden and crispy. Add the diced pork sausage to the potatoes and cook until golden. Remember, colour means flavour. Season with the salt and smoked paprika and fry for a further 10 seconds, then remove from the heat and mix in the chopped coriander.

3 Place the tortilla onto a flat surface. Mix the cheeses and sprinkle over one half of the tortilla, leaving about 1cm around the edges. Scatter the potato and sausage hash over the cheese and fold over the other half of the tortilla, creating a half-moon shape.

4 Heat a large, non-stick frying pan over medium heat. Carefully place the quesadilla into the pan and allow it to toast gently to a beautiful golden-brown colour. Flip over and cook the other side. Place the toasted quesadilla onto a chopping board and cut in half.

QUESADILLAS AND ENCHILADAS

PORK QUESADILLA

SERVES 2

canola oil for frying

2kg pork shoulder, deboned

salt and ground black pepper to taste

100g spicy sesame marinade (page 24)

1 x store-bought 25cm flour tortilla

¼ cup grated cheddar cheese

¼ cup grated mozzarella cheese

2 batches quesadilla filling (page 56)

garlic mayo (page 28)

fresh coriander for garnishing

1 Preheat the oven to 190°C. On the stovetop, heat a little canola oil in a heavy-based ovenproof pot over medium heat.

2 Season the pork shoulder with salt and black pepper and place it into the pot. Brown it on all sides until a deep golden colour, then remove the pork from the pot and rub it all over with the spicy sesame marinade. Return the pork to the pot and add some water to cover about a quarter of the shoulder.

3 Put on the lid and place the pot in the oven for 2.5–3 hours, checking the water level every 30 minutes. Top up with a little more water if needed.

4 When cooked, transfer the pork shoulder to a tray to cool slightly.

5 Return the pot to the stovetop over medium heat and reduce the liquid until thick. While the sauce reduces, shred the pork into a bowl. When thickened, strain the sauce through a sieve into the bowl with the pulled pork. Mix gently and check for seasoning.

6 Place the tortilla onto a flat surface. Mix the cheeses and sprinkle over one half of the tortilla, leaving about 1cm around the edges. Scatter the pulled pork over the cheese and cover with the quesadilla filling. Add dollops of garlic mayo and then fold over the other half of the tortilla, creating a half-moon shape.

7 Heat a large, non-stick frying pan over medium heat. Carefully place the quesadilla into the pan and allow it to toast gently to a beautiful golden-brown colour. Flip over and cook the other side. Place the toasted quesadilla onto a chopping board, cut in half and garnish with fresh coriander.

CHICKEN QUESADILLA

SERVES **2**

4 deboned skinless chicken thighs

½ cup lime and coriander marinade (page 17)

1 x store-bought 25cm flour tortilla

¼ cup grated cheddar cheese

¼ cup grated mozzarella cheese

2 batches quesadilla filling (page 56)

smoky chipotle mayo (page 29)

fresh coriander for garnishing

1 Marinate the chicken thighs in the lime and coriander marinade for about 5 minutes.

2 In a dry, heavy-based frying pan over medium heat, cook the marinated chicken thighs, skin-side down, for 10–12 minutes, then flip them over to cook the other side. Keep basting the thighs until browned and cooked through. Remove the thighs from the pan and allow them to rest and cool before cutting into bite-size chunks.

3 Place the tortilla onto a flat surface. Mix the cheeses and sprinkle over one half of the tortilla, leaving about 1cm around the edges. Scatter the cooked chicken over the cheese and cover with the quesadilla filling. Add dollops of smoky chipotle mayo and then fold over the other half of the tortilla, creating a half-moon shape.

4 Heat a large, non-stick frying pan over medium heat. Carefully place the quesadilla into the pan and allow it to toast gently to a beautiful golden-brown colour. Flip over and cook the other side. Place the toasted quesadilla onto a chopping board, cut in half and garnish with fresh coriander.

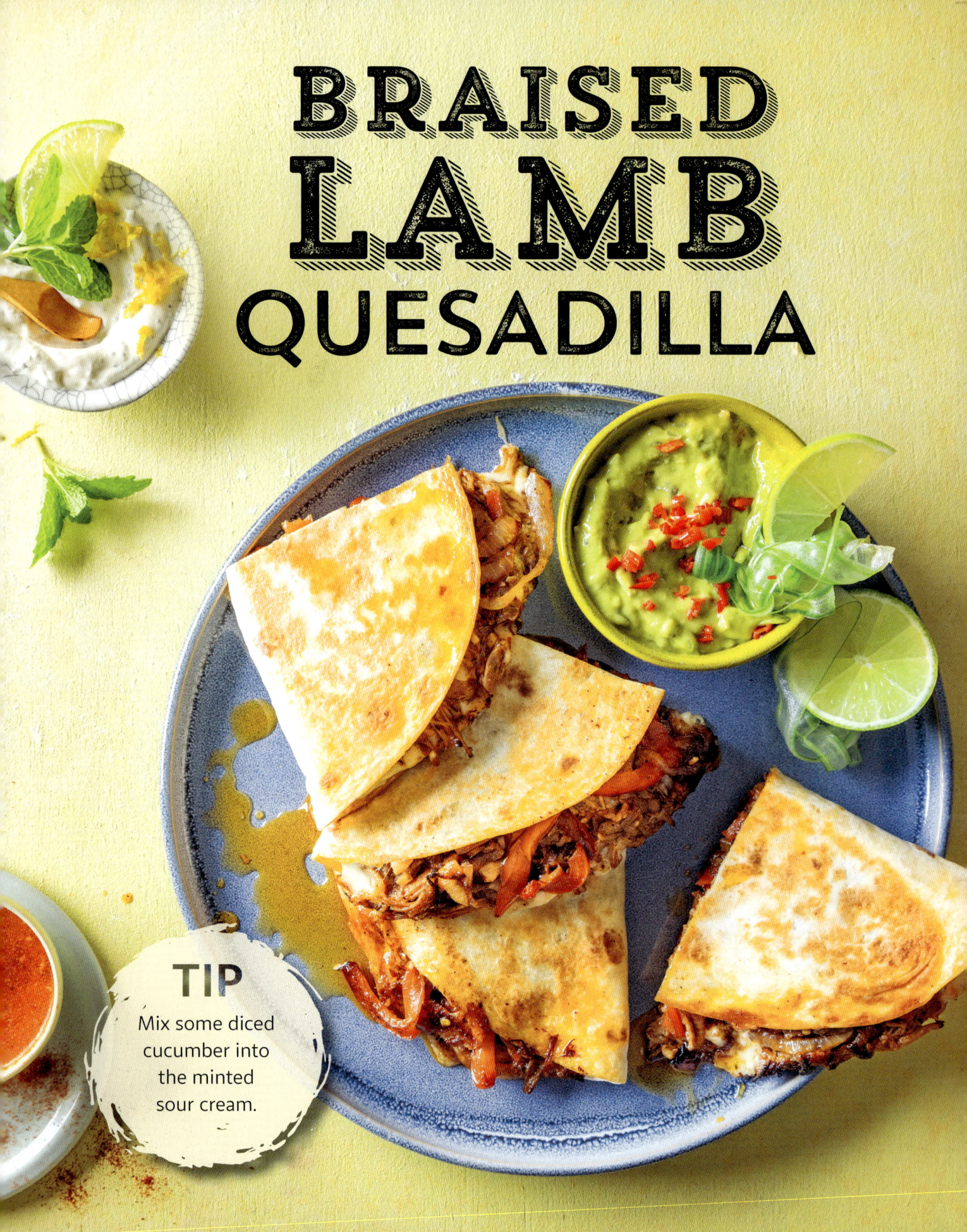

BRAISED LAMB QUESADILLA

TIP Mix some diced cucumber into the minted sour cream.

SERVES **2**

canola oil for frying

4 large red onions, roughly diced

2kg lamb shoulder, deboned

salt and ground black pepper to taste

½ cup lamb marinade (page 25)

1 x store-bought 25cm flour tortilla

¼ cup grated cheddar cheese

¼ cup grated mozzarella cheese

2 batches quesadilla filling (page 56)

fresh coriander for garnishing

guacamole (page 18) or minted sour cream (page 47)

1 Preheat the oven to 190°C.

2 On the stovetop, heat a little canola oil in a heavy-based ovenproof pot over medium heat. Add the red onions and fry until light golden brown. Remove the onions from the pot and set aside.

3 Season the lamb shoulder with salt and black pepper and place it into the pot. Brown it on all sides until a deep golden colour, then remove the lamb from the pot and rub it all over with the lamb marinade. Return the lamb to the pot along with the onions and add some water to cover about a quarter of the shoulder.

4 Put on the lid and place the pot in the oven for 2.5–3 hours, checking the water level every 30 minutes. Top up with a little more water if needed.

5 When cooked, transfer the lamb shoulder to a tray to cool slightly.

6 Return the pot to the stovetop over medium heat and reduce the liquid until thick. While the sauce reduces, shred the lamb into a bowl. When thickened, strain the sauce through a sieve into the bowl with the shredded lamb. Mix gently and check for seasoning.

7 Place the tortilla onto a flat surface. Mix the cheeses and sprinkle over one half of the tortilla, leaving about 1cm around the edges. Scatter the shredded lamb over the cheese and cover with the quesadilla filling. Fold over the other half of the tortilla, creating a half-moon shape.

8 Heat a large, non-stick frying pan over medium heat. Carefully place the quesadilla into the pan and allow it to toast gently to a beautiful golden-brown colour. Flip over and cook the other side. Place the toasted quesadilla onto a chopping board, cut in half and garnish with fresh coriander. Serve the guacamole or minted sour cream on the side.

QUESADILLAS AND ENCHILADAS

ENCHILADA SAUCE

This recipe forms the base for all the enchiladas in this book.

MAKES 1 CUP

- 2 Tbsp olive oil
- 1 clove garlic
- ¼ tsp ground turmeric
- 2 tsp red chilli flakes
- 6 dried curry leaves
- 2 Tbsp tomato paste
- 1 x 410g can tomato purée
- ½ cup double cream
- 1 tsp salt
- 1 tsp ground black pepper
- 1 tsp origanum
- 1 tsp white sugar

1 Heat the olive oil in a large frying pan over low heat. Add the garlic, turmeric, chilli flakes and curry leaves and cook for 1 minute.

2 Add the tomato paste and cook for a further 30 seconds. Make sure the spices don't burn. When you can smell the beautiful curry aroma, add the tomato purée, cream, salt, pepper, origanum and sugar.

3 Bring to a light simmer and cook for 15–20 minutes. If it's looking too dry, add a tablespoon of water during cooking. The sauce should have the viscosity of a thin soup. Remove the curry leaves before using.

BEEF
ENCHILADAS

SERVES 4–6

canola oil for frying

2kg whole beef brisket, bone in

salt and ground black pepper to taste

½ cup beef spice rub (page 23)

12–15 corn tortillas (page 11)

1 cup enchilada sauce (page 64)

¼ cup grated cheddar cheese

¼ cup grated mozzarella cheese

fresh coriander for garnishing

1 Preheat the oven to 190°C.

2 On the stovetop, heat a little canola oil in a heavy-based ovenproof pot over medium heat.

3 Season the beef brisket with salt and black pepper and place it into the pot. Brown it on all sides until a deep golden colour, then remove the beef from the pot and rub it all over with the spice rub. Return the beef to the pot and add some water to cover about a quarter of the brisket.

4 Put on the lid and place the pot in the oven for 2.5–3 hours, checking the water level every 30 minutes. Top up with a little more water if needed. The beef brisket is cooked when you can pull out the bone and it comes out clean.

5 When cooked, transfer the beef brisket to a tray to cool slightly.

6 Return the pot to the stovetop over medium heat and reduce the liquid until thick. While the sauce reduces, shred the beef into a bowl. When thickened, strain the sauce through a sieve into the bowl with the shredded beef. Mix gently and check for seasoning.

7 Reheat the oven to 180°C.

8 Place a tortilla onto a flat surface. Place a healthy amount of shredded beef in a line in the centre of the tortilla, then roll it up like a pancake to encase the filling completely. Repeat with the remaining tortillas.

9 Place the rolled tortillas into an ovenproof dish, seam-side down, in a single layer. Spoon over the enchilada sauce, spreading it evenly to cover the tortillas. Mix the cheeses and distribute evenly over the sauce.

10 Bake for 20–25 minutes on the middle rack of the oven until the cheese has melted and the sauce is bubbling. Garnish with fresh coriander.

BRAISED LAMB ENCHILADAS

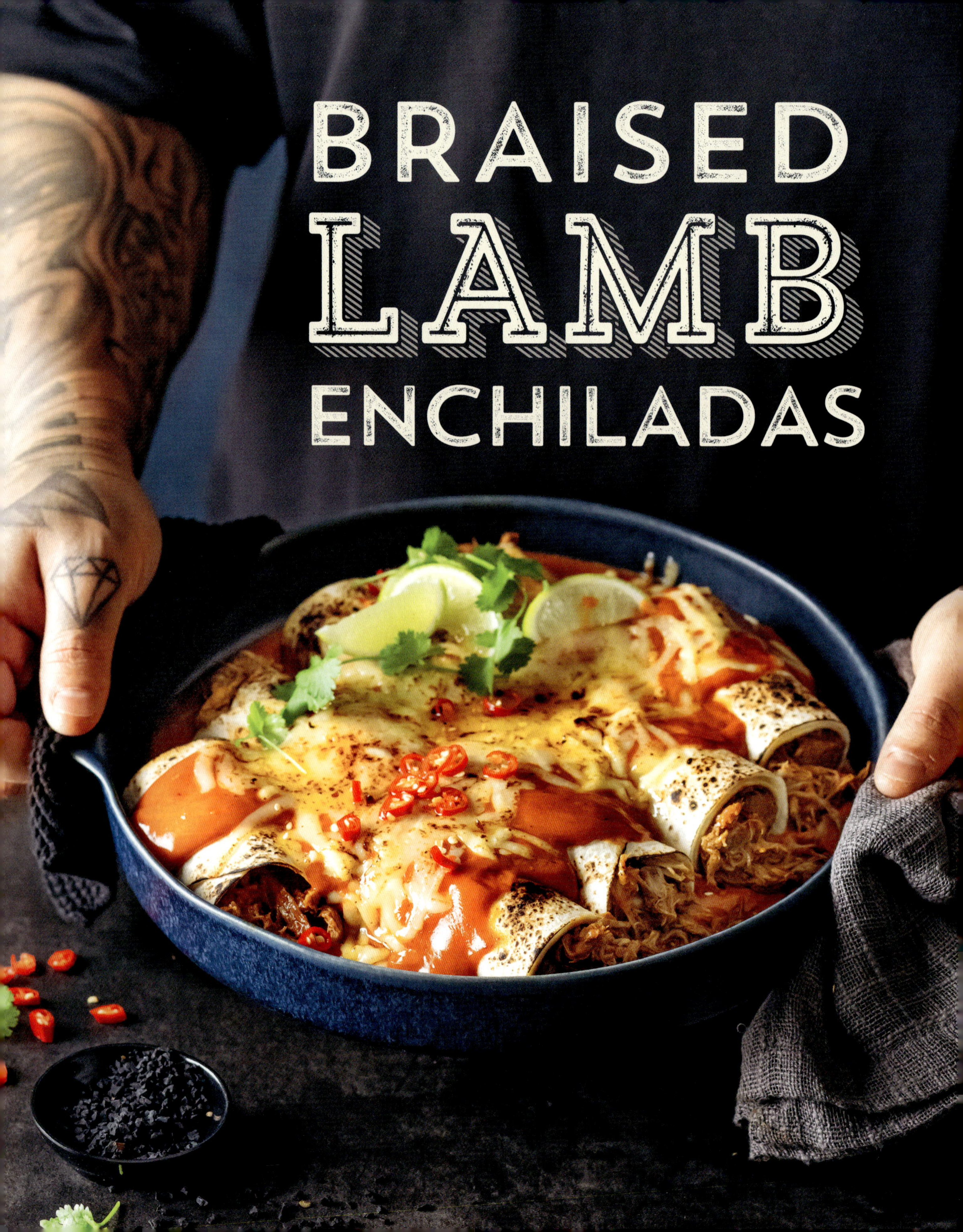

SERVES 4–6

canola oil for frying

2kg lamb shoulder, deboned

salt and ground black pepper to taste

½ cup lamb marinade (page 25)

4 large red onions, roughly diced

12–15 corn tortillas (page 11)

1 cup enchilada sauce (page 64)

¼ cup grated cheddar cheese

¼ cup grated mozzarella cheese

fresh coriander for garnishing

1 Preheat the oven to 190°C.

2 On the stovetop, heat a little canola oil in a heavy-based ovenproof pot over medium heat. Add the red onions and fry until light golden brown. Remove the onions from the pot and set aside.

3 Season the lamb shoulder with salt and black pepper and place it into the pot. Brown it on all sides until a deep golden colour, then remove the lamb from the pot and rub it all over with the lamb marinade. Return the lamb along with the onions to the pot and add some water to cover about a quarter of the shoulder.

4 Put on the lid and place the pot in the oven for 2.5–3 hours, checking the water level every 30 minutes. Top up with a little more water if needed.

5 When cooked, transfer the lamb shoulder to a tray to cool slightly.

6 Return the pot to the stovetop over medium heat and reduce the liquid until thick. While the sauce reduces, shred the lamb into a bowl. When thickened, strain the sauce through a sieve into the bowl with the shredded lamb. Mix gently and check for seasoning.

7 Reheat the oven to 180°C.

8 Place a tortilla onto a flat surface. Place a healthy amount of shredded lamb in a line in the centre of the tortilla, then roll it up like a pancake to encase the filling completely. Repeat with the remaining tortillas.

9 Place the rolled tortillas into an ovenproof dish, seam-side down, in a single layer. Spoon over the enchilada sauce, spreading it evenly to cover the tortillas. Mix the cheeses and distribute evenly over the sauce.

10 Bake for 20–25 minutes on the middle rack of the oven until the cheese has melted and the sauce is bubbling. Garnish with fresh coriander.

PULLED PORK ENCHILADAS

SERVES **4–6**

canola oil for frying
2kg whole pork shoulder, deboned
salt and ground black pepper to taste
50g spicy sesame marinade (page 24)
12–15 corn tortillas (page 11)
1 cup enchilada sauce (page 64)
¼ cup grated cheddar cheese
¼ cup grated mozzarella cheese
fresh coriander for garnishing

1 Preheat the oven to 190°C. On the stovetop, heat a little canola oil in a heavy-based ovenproof pot over medium heat.

2 Season the pork shoulder with salt and black pepper and place it into the pot. Brown it on all sides until a deep golden colour, then remove the pork from the pot and rub it all over with the spicy sesame marinade. Return the pork to the pot and add some water to cover about a quarter of the shoulder.

3 Put on the lid and place the pot in the oven for 2.5–3 hours, checking the water level every 30 minutes. Top up with a little more water if needed.

4 When cooked, transfer the pork shoulder to a tray to cool slightly.

5 Return the pot to the stovetop over medium heat and reduce the liquid until thick. While the sauce reduces, shred the pork into a bowl. When thickened, strain the sauce through a sieve into the bowl with the pulled pork. Mix gently and check for seasoning.

6 Reheat the oven to 180°C.

7 Place a tortilla onto a flat surface. Place a healthy amount of shredded pork in a line in the centre of the tortilla, then roll it up like a pancake to encase the filling completely. Repeat with the remaining tortillas.

8 Place the rolled tortillas into an ovenproof dish, seam-side down, in a single layer. Spoon over the enchilada sauce, spreading it evenly to cover the tortillas. Mix the cheeses and distribute evenly over the sauce.

9 Bake for 20–25 minutes on the middle rack of the oven until the cheese has melted and the sauce is bubbling. Garnish with fresh coriander.

TIP
You can get orange pepper spice from any Indian market or spice shop.

MASALA POTATO ENCHILADAS

SERVES **4**

3 large potatoes, peeled
50g butter
1 clove garlic, finely chopped
3 Tbsp orange pepper spice
salt to taste
1½ Tbsp chopped fresh coriander
12–15 corn tortillas (page 11)
1 cup enchilada sauce (page 64)
¼ cup grated cheddar cheese
¼ cup grated mozzarella cheese
fresh coriander for garnishing

1 Boil the potatoes in a pot of water until firm but fork tender. Strain and allow to cool, then cut into bite-size chunks.

2 Melt the butter in a large frying pan over medium heat. When it starts to foam, add the garlic and orange pepper spice and cook for 1 minute. Add the potato chunks, mix well and turn up the heat to get some colour on the spuds. Season with salt and cook until the potatoes are completely tender. Remove the pan from the heat and gently mix in the chopped coriander.

3 Preheat the oven to 180°C.

4 Place a tortilla onto a flat surface. Place a healthy amount of masala potato in a line in the centre of the tortilla, then roll it up like a pancake to encase the filling completely. Repeat with the remaining tortillas.

5 Place the rolled tortillas into an ovenproof dish, seam-side down, in a single layer. Spoon over the enchilada sauce, spreading it evenly to cover the tortillas. Mix the cheeses and distribute evenly over the sauce.

6 Bake for 20–25 minutes on the middle rack of the oven until the cheese has melted and the sauce is bubbling. Garnish with fresh coriander.

TAPAS

Tapas consists of small plates of a variety of different foods, from vegetarian to meat-based dishes that are meant to be shared. In Central America, these are referred to as *boca*.

CHILLI CON CARNE

When it comes to making chilli con carne, what ingredient goes in when is very important to achieve the best result.

SERVES 4

¼ cup canola oil
2 medium white onions, chopped
2 cloves garlic, finely chopped
500g beef mince
salt to taste
50g tomato paste
2 tsp ground cumin
1 tsp cayenne pepper
1 tsp smoked paprika
2 tsp white sugar
150ml dry red wine
1 x 410g can chopped peeled tomatoes
1 x 410g can kidney beans
20g cheddar cheese, grated
10g raw white onion, chopped
1½ Tbsp chopped fresh coriander
4 tsp sour cream

1 Heat the canola oil in a large, heavy-based, preferably cast-iron, pot over medium heat. Add the onions and garlic and sauté until the onions become translucent, then remove from the pot and set aside.

2 Add the mince to the same pot, breaking it up with a spoon. Season with salt and cook the mince until it turns a deep, golden brown; this will take some time and patience, but colour means flavour. When you have reached this point, return the onion and garlic to the pan.

3 Add the tomato paste and mix well. Continue stirring for about 20 seconds to cook out the sharp bitter notes from the tomato. Next, add the cumin, cayenne pepper, paprika and sugar and give it a quick stir.

4 Pour in the red wine and allow it to cook until almost completely evaporated, then add the canned tomatoes and the kidney beans, liquid and all. Stir gently to combine, then turn down the heat to low, cover with a lid and leave to simmer for at least 30 minutes, stirring occasionally. The chilli is done when it is thick, rich and dark in colour. Check the seasoning – you may need to add a little more salt.

5 Spoon the chilli con carne into a serving bowl, sprinkle over the grated cheese and raw chopped onion, garnish with the chopped coriander and dollop the sour cream in the middle.

MEXICAN-STYLE RICE

SERVES 4

150g uncooked white rice
1 Tbsp canola oil
70g white onion, sliced
50g grilled corn kernels
1 tsp chilli flakes
1 tsp ground cumin
½ x 410g can kidney beans, drained
¾ tsp salt
1½ Tbsp chopped fresh coriander

1 Cook the rice in a pot of salted water until soft and tender. Strain and allow to drain in a colander for 5 minutes.

2 Heat the canola oil in a large, heavy-based saucepan over high heat. When the oil starts to shimmer, add the onion and grilled corn and cook for about 1 minute to get some colour.

3 Add the chilli flakes, cumin and cooked rice and sauté until the rice takes on the colour of the spices.

4 Add the kidney beans and cook, stirring occasionally, for a further 2 minutes to dry out the mixture. Add the salt, transfer to a serving bowl and garnish with the fresh coriander.

TIP
When cooking white rice, use a ratio of 1:2, e.g. 1 cup rice to 2 cups water or 100g rice to 200g water.

MEXICAN-STYLE RICE

CHILLI CON CARNE

TIP

Jalapeños vary. If they are not as hot as you would like, add some chopped chillies to the cheese filling.

JALAPEÑO CHILLI POPPERS

SERVES 2

30g mozzarella cheese, grated
30g cheddar cheese, grated
3 tsp salt
½ tsp ground black pepper
1 Tbsp crème fraiche
1 cup cake flour
½ cup beer or sparkling water
1 Tbsp canola oil
4–6 cups sunflower oil
3–4 large jalapeño chillies

1 To make the filling, combine the cheeses in a bowl, add 1 tsp salt and the pepper and mix well. Add the crème fraiche and mix until it comes together like dough. Alternatively, blend everything in a food processor until it comes together.

2 Place the flour and remaining salt in a bowl, followed by the beer or sparkling water and the canola oil, and whisk until smooth. If the batter is too runny, add a bit more flour. If it is too thick, add a bit more liquid.

3 Heat the sunflower oil to 190°C in a heavy-based pot.

4 Make a slit in the jalapeño chillies lengthways and remove the seeds – try your best to keep the stems on.

5 Stuff the jalapeños with as much filling as you can, then, holding them by their stems, dip them into the batter. Allow any excess batter to drip off before placing them into the hot oil.

6 Fry until golden brown and crispy, then remove from the oil and drain on paper towel. Enjoy immediately with sour cream, guacamole or any other sauce of your choosing.

TAPAS

DEEP-FRIED AVOCADO

This is something outside the box. Like most good things, it came about quite by accident. There is no in-between with this one. It's either 'yes' you like it, or 'no' you don't ... but please just give it a try. Remember to serve it hot, crispy and fresh!

SERVES 2

4–6 cups sunflower oil

20g cake flour

½ tsp salt, plus extra for sprinkling

¼ tsp ground black pepper

1 egg, beaten

80g panko crumbs

1 avocado, cut into 6–8 wedges

3–4 Tbsp chipotle chilli marinade (page 16)

200ml sour cream

1 Heat the sunflower oil to 190°C in a heavy-based pot.

2 Mix the flour, salt and pepper in a small bowl. Place the beaten egg in a second bowl and the panko crumbs in a third.

3 Coat the avocado wedges in the seasoned flour, shake off any excess, then dip them into the beaten egg. Once covered in egg, put them straight into the panko crumbs and ensure they are well coated.

4 Fry the crumbed avocado wedges until golden and crispy, then remove from the oil and drain on paper towel. Sprinkle with salt.

5 Mix the chipotle chilli marinade into the sour cream to make a dipping sauce for the crispy avo wedges.

TIP

Use an avocado that is slightly firm to the touch; this will make it easier to cut into wedges.

CRISPY CALAMARI

SERVES 2

1 cup rice flour or cornflour

2 Tbsp shichimi togarashi (Japanese seven spice)

1 tsp salt, plus extra for sprinkling

4–6 cups sunflower oil

240g calamari tubes, cleaned

pickled chilli mayo (page 28)

1. Mix the flour, shichimi togarashi and salt in a small bowl.

2. Heat some sunflower oil to 190°C in a heavy-based pot.

3. Coat the calamari tubes in the seasoned flour, shake off any excess and gently put them into the oil. Fry the calamari tubes until they turn a light cream colour – do not overcook.

4. Remove the calamari from the oil, drain on paper towel and sprinkle with salt. Enjoy immediately with pickled chilli mayo.

TIP

Serve some fried pickled red chilli alongside the calamari to add colour to the finished dish.

CREAMY CORN BOWL

Cheesy, gooey goodness perfect for a cold winter's day. My first experience of a creamy corn bowl was sitting in front of the fire under a cosy blanket, watching a movie. It is a memory I will never forget.

SERVES 2

2 Tbsp canola oil
100g whole corn kernels
½ tsp salt
2 Tbsp chopped fresh coriander
15g mozzarella cheese, grated
20g feta cheese, crumbled
1 Tbsp sliced spring onion
½ tsp thinly sliced red chilli
1 Tbsp chopped fresh mint
fresh coriander for garnishing

BÉCHAMEL SAUCE

2 Tbsp butter
2 Tbsp cake flour
1¼ cups milk
1 tsp salt

1 First make the béchamel sauce. Melt the butter in a heavy-based saucepan, stir in the flour and cook until the paste bubbles slightly. Add the milk, a little at a time, stirring continuously. As the sauce starts to thicken, add the salt and lower the heat. Cook for a further 5 minutes, stirring occasionally. Remove from the heat and allow to cool.

2 Heat the canola oil in a frying pan. When the oil starts to smoke, add the corn kernels and cook until tender but still firm.

3 Add the salt, coriander and 2 Tbsp béchamel sauce.

4 Add a splash of water to loosen the mixture, if necessary, then stir in the mozzarella cheese.

5 Once the cheese has melted, remove the pan from the heat and spoon the creamy corn into a serving bowl.

6 Top with the feta cheese, spring onion, red chilli and mint leaves. Garnish with fresh coriander.

TIP
Leftover béchamel sauce can be kept in the fridge in an airtight container for up to 3 days.

MEXICAN-STYLE FRIES

Let's be honest, not everyone has time to make their own chips, which is why it's perfectly acceptable to use store-bought thick-cut frozen chips here. If you are making your own hand-cut chips, make sure you parboil them first; do not fry them raw.

SERVES 2

4–6 cups sunflower oil

100g frozen chips or 2 medium potatoes, peeled, cut into chips and parboiled

1 tsp canola oil

1 Tbsp chopped garlic

1 Tbsp chopped chilli

½ tsp salt

¼ tsp cayenne pepper

¼ tsp smoked paprika

½ lemon

¼ cup chopped fresh coriander

garlic mayo (page 28)

1 Heat the sunflower oil to 180°C in a heavy-based pot and fry the chips until crispy and dark golden brown.

2 Heat the canola oil in a large frying pan over medium heat. When the oil starts to shimmer, add the garlic and chilli and fry for 10 seconds.

3 Drain the chips and add them to the pan, stirring to ensure they are well coated.

4 Add the salt, cayenne pepper and paprika, shaking the pan to coat the chips, then squeeze over the lemon juice.

5 Garnish with the chopped coriander and serve immediately with garlic mayo.

FISH CEVICHE

*Think summer – the sun is shining,
you're sitting poolside with a margarita in one hand
and a bowl of ceviche with corn chips in the other. A match made in heaven.*

SERVES **4**

200g fresh white fish, cut into bite-size pieces

100g avocado, cut into bite-size pieces

2 Tbsp lemon juice

¾ tsp salt

¼ tsp ground black pepper

¼ tsp cayenne pepper

4 dashes Tabasco sauce

4 dashes Worcestershire sauce

30g pineapple or mango, diced (optional)

100g pico de gallo (page 14)

60g corn chips

1 Place the fish and avocado in a bowl and add the lemon juice. Mix gently but well, then season with the salt, black pepper and cayenne pepper and give it another good mix. Add the Tabasco and Worcestershire sauces and give it a final mix.

2 Add the pineapple or mango, if using, and the pico de gallo and give it a final stir to combine.

3 Taste the ceviche – by now the fish should have turned opaque and taken on a nice balance of salty and sour. Adjust seasoning if needed.

4 Serve the corn chips on the side to scoop up the ceviche.

TIPS

Enjoy the ceviche the same day – don't marinate the fish in the lemon juice for too long, as it will turn mushy. You can use any white flesh fish, but if you're skittish about raw fish, you can use cooked prawns or shrimp instead.

PERI CITRUS PRAWNS

SERVES **2**

¼ cup lime and coriander marinade (page 17)

2 Tbsp Mexican-style durky sauce (page 26)

2 Tbsp canola oil

6 large tiger prawns, shell on, butterflied and deveined

20g cashew nuts, roasted and chopped

fresh coriander for garnishing

1 lime, cut into wedges

1 In a bowl, mix the lime and coriander marinade with the durky sauce.

2 Heat the canola oil in a large frying pan, then place the prawns, flesh-side down, into the pan and cook until the flesh turns opaque and slightly pink. Flip them over and cook the other side until the entire prawn turns pink.

3 Turn down the heat and add the sauce. Using a spoon, baste the prawns in the sauce until well coated.

4 Serve the prawns sprinkled with the cashews and fresh coriander and the lime wedges on the side.

CRISPY QUINOA SALAD

This is another crowd pleaser. The flavours are quite complex, and the addition of honey might seem strange, but somehow it just works.

SERVES 4

- 1 cup uncooked quinoa
- 2 Tbsp olive oil
- 2 tsp salt
- 120g avocado, cut into bite-size chunks
- 40g drained kidney beans
- 50g grilled corn kernels
- ¼ cup pico de gallo (page 14)
- fresh coriander for garnishing

QUINOA SALAD DRESSING

- juice of 2 large lemons
- 2 Tbsp honey
- 2 cloves garlic, minced
- 2 Tbsp chopped fresh coriander
- 2 tsp shichimi togarashi (Japanese seven spice)
- ¼ cup cold water
- salt to taste

1 Place a pot of salted water over medium heat, add the quinoa and bring to a simmer. Cook for 15–20 minutes until tender, then carefully drain and allow to cool slightly in the pot.

2 Preheat the oven to 190°C and line a baking tray with greaseproof paper.

3 Add the olive oil and salt to the pot and run your fingers through the quinoa to coat it.

4 Evenly spread the quinoa in a single layer on the lined baking tray to avoid clumping.

5 Bake for 35 minutes, mixing every 10 minutes, until the quinoa is golden brown and crispy.

6 Place the avocado, kidney beans, grilled corn and pico de gallo into a salad bowl.

7 Combine all the ingredients for the quinoa salad dressing in a separate bowl, whisking well.

8 Pour 2 Tbsp of the dressing over the salad and mix gently so as not to squash the avocado. Check and adjust seasoning, if necessary.

9 Sprinkle 1 Tbsp of the crispy quinoa over the top, but do not mix it in, and garnish with fresh coriander.

TIP

'The remaining crispy quinoa can be stored at room temperature in an airtight glass jar for up to 2 weeks. The quinoa salad dressing can be stored in the fridge in an airtight container for up to a week.

CHILLI CON CARNE VETKOEK

Mexican vetkoek just sounds right. Plus, it lends itself to many different filling and sauce combinations, so mix and match according to your cravings, from lamb and mint to masala potatoes and coriander, the options are endless.

SERVES 6

1 cup lukewarm water
2 Tbsp white sugar
5g active dry yeast
3½ cups white bread flour
1 tsp salt
1½ cups sunflower oil
1 cup guacamole (page 18)
2 cups chilli con carne (page 76)
½ cup sour cream
fresh coriander for garnishing

1 Mix the lukewarm water, sugar and yeast in a small bowl. Let it stand for about 5 minutes or until the yeast starts to bubble.

2 Mix the flour and salt in a separate large bowl, then pour over the wet mixture. Knead until a smooth, elastic dough forms (this can be done in a stand mixer).

3 Cover the bowl with a clean, damp cloth and leave the dough to rise until doubled in size.

4 Knock back the dough and portion it into 120g balls. Flatten the dough balls using the palm of your hand and set aside on a floured surface.

5 Heat the sunflower oil in a large heavy-based pot to 175°C and fry the dough rounds for about 3 minutes on each side until golden brown. Drain on paper towel and allow to cool.

6 When the vetkoek are cool enough to handle, cut them in half horizontally three-quarters of the way through. Spread some guacamole inside the vetkoek, spoon in some warm chilli con carne and a dollop of sour cream and garnish with fresh coriander.

TAPAS

PLAIN NACHOS

Although nachos are technically Tex-Mex and not authentic Mexican, they're still a must-have on any Mexican menu. The secret to great nachos is to use corn chips, a generous amount of cheese, fresh guacamole and a good sour cream. The end result should be a beautiful mosaic of red, white and green.

SERVES **4**

60g mozzarella cheese, grated
60g cheddar cheese, grated
120g corn chips
80g guacamole (page 18)
50g sour cream
¼ cup pico de gallo (page 14)
fresh coriander for garnishing

1 Preheat the oven to 190°C and mix the cheeses together in a bowl.

2 Place a layer of corn chips on the bottom of an ovenproof dish, evenly sprinkle over some cheese and place another layer of corn chips on top. Repeat the layers until you have used all the corn chips and cheese, finishing with a thick layer of cheese.

3 Bake for 8–10 minutes or until all the cheese has melted.

4 Remove from the oven and top with nice big dollops of guacamole and sour cream. Scatter the pico de gallo over the top and garnish with fresh coriander.

> **VARIATION: ADD SOME PROTEIN**
> Use the nachos recipe as a base and add a protein of your choice, such as lime and coriander chicken (page 34), chilli con carne (page 76), braised lamb shoulder (page 47) or beef brisket (page 42).

TIP

For a different flavour profile, use roasted corn salsa (page 14) as an alternative to pico de gallo.

CRISPY CHICKEN WINGS

SERVES 2

6 chicken wings
2 eggs, beaten
50g cake flour
2 tsp salt, plus extra for sprinkling
1 tsp ground black pepper
150g puffed rice cereal
4–6 cups sunflower oil
50ml sour cream
100ml Mexican-style durky sauce (page 26)

1. Cut each chicken wing into the wingette and drumette.

2. Place the beaten eggs in one bowl, the flour, salt and pepper in another and the puffed rice cereal in a third.

3. Coat the chicken pieces in the seasoned flour, dust off any excess flour and place them directly into the beaten egg. Once covered in the egg, put them straight into the puffed rice cereal and cover them completely; you can give them a squeeze to ensure the rice cereal sticks.

4. Heat the sunflower oil in a large heavy-based pot to 160°C and fry the chicken pieces until golden and crispy. Drain on paper towel and sprinkle with salt.

5. Serve the wings with the sour cream and durky sauce on the side for dipping.

TIPS
Check the doneness of each chicken wing, as they vary in size. Alternatively, boil them in salted water before frying.

The air fryer has become massively popular all over the world for its convenience and health benefits, and there's plenty of scope for some quick and easy Mexican recipes for those busy workdays. You might need a pan here or there, but the air fryer will do most of the work for you. Allow your imagination to run wild, use your initiative and pair the salsas, meats and sauces that work best for you. There are no limits!

MEXICAN TOSTADAS

Use a protein and salsa of your choice. Try pulled beef brisket (page 42), pulled pork (page 45) or lime and coriander chicken (page 34) with pico de gallo (page 14), roasted corn salsa (page 14) or roasted tomato salsa (page 106).

200°C | 6 MINUTES

SERVES **2**

2 x store-bought 12cm soft flour tortillas

1 Tbsp olive oil

¼ cup guacamole (page 18)

150g protein of choice

2 Tbsp salsa of choice

20g Greek feta cheese

fresh coriander for garnishing

1 Preheat the air fryer to 200°C.

2 Brush one side of the flour tortillas with the olive oil. Place them into the air fryer, oil-side up, and weigh them down with a small sauce bowl. Cook for the full 6 minutes or until they turn golden and crispy. They might bend and buckle, but this is completely normal. Once done, take them out of the air fryer and allow to cool completely.

3 Spread a layer of guacamole on each tostada. Spoon a healthy amount of your chosen protein onto the guacamole and spread it out, leaving some space around the edges. Top with a spoon of your chosen salsa, crumble over the feta and garnish with fresh coriander.

MEXICO MEETS AIR FRYER

ROASTED TOMATO SALSA

200°C | 10 MINUTES

MAKES 1 CUP

3 ripe tomatoes
1 jalapeño chilli, deseeded
¼ red onion, peeled
1 Tbsp olive oil
salt to taste
1 small clove garlic, finely chopped
3 Tbsp fresh coriander
juice of 1 lime

1 Preheat the air fryer to 200°C.

2 Rub the tomatoes, jalapeño chilli and red onion with the olive oil and season with salt. Place them into the air fryer and cook for 10 minutes, giving the basket a shake every now and then. When the vegetables are blistered and soft, remove them from the air fryer and allow to cool.

3 Remove the skin of the tomatoes and place all the ingredients into a food processor, NOT a blender. Pulse to form a semi-chunky salsa – it mustn't be too smooth. Check and adjust seasoning – you may need to add a touch more salt and lime juice.

MEXICAN-STYLE STREET CORN

200°C | 8 MINUTES

SERVES 4

- 2 corn cobs
- 2 Tbsp mayonnaise
- 1 tsp smoked paprika
- ¼ cup finely grated parmesan, cotija or Greek feta cheese
- 1 tsp chilli powder
- fresh coriander for garnishing
- 1 lime wedge

1. Place a large pot of cold salted water over high heat, add the corn cobs and bring to the boil. When the water reaches a rolling boil, remove the corn cobs from the pot and set aside to cool.

2. Preheat the air fryer to 200°C.

3. In a small bowl, mix the mayonnaise and smoked paprika. Break the corn cobs in half to fit into the air fryer. Using a pastry brush or butter knife, smear the mayonnaise mixture over the corn cobs, making sure they are covered.

4. Place the corn cobs into the air fryer and cook for 8 minutes, turning halfway. They are done when the corn kernels are soft and slightly blistered.

5. Remove the corn cobs from the air fryer, brush them with a little more mayo and immediately roll them in the cheese until completely covered.

6. Place the corn cobs on a serving dish, dust with the chilli powder, garnish with fresh coriander and enjoy with a squeeze of fresh lime juice.

CRISPY MEXICAN TAQUITOS

A taquito, or rolled taco, typically consists of a small tortilla rolled around a filling. Use a protein of your choice. I recommend pulled beef brisket (page 42) or pulled pork (page 45).

200°C | 6 MINUTES

SERVES **2**

4 x store-bought 12cm soft flour tortillas

1 Tbsp olive oil

250g protein of choice

50g mozzarella cheese, grated

guacamole (page 18)

1 Preheat the air fryer to 200°C.

2 Brush one side of a flour tortilla with the olive oil. Lay the tortilla, oil-side down, on a work surface. Place about a quarter of the protein of your choice on the end of the tortilla closest to you, as much as you think you can fit, and sprinkle a quarter of the cheese on top. Roll the tortilla like a pancake and set aside while you make the rest.

3 Place the prepped taquitos into the air fryer, seam-side down, and cook for the full 6 minutes.

4 They are done when they turn a crisp, light golden brown and the cheese has melted.

5 Serve with some guacamole on the side.

Serve with Mexican-style rice (page 77) for a complete meal.

200°C | 12–15 MINUTES

SERVES **2**

30g mozzarella cheese, grated
30g cheddar cheese, grated
2 jalapeño chillies, deseeded and finely chopped
1 tsp salt
½ tsp ground black pepper
1 Tbsp crème fraiche
2 deboned chicken breasts, skin on
salt and ground black pepper to taste
¼ cup chipotle chilli marinade (page 16)

1 Preheat the air fryer to 200°C.

2 To make the filling, combine the cheeses and chopped jalapeño chillies in a bowl, add the salt and pepper and mix well. Add the crème fraiche and mix until it comes together like dough. Alternatively, blend everything in a food processor until it comes together.

3 Lay the chicken breasts on a cutting board. Using a sharp knife, butterfly the breasts horizontally starting at the thicker end.

4 Season both sides with salt and black pepper and place the breasts, skin-side down, on a flat surface. Place 2 Tbsp of the jalapeño mixture in a line in the centre of each butterflied chicken breast.

5 Beginning at the long end, fold the chicken over the filling, covering it completely, and then continue rolling to create a cigar shape. Secure with 3 or 4 skewers. Repeat with the second chicken breast.

6 Place the breasts, seam-side down and skin-side up, into the air fryer. Brush lightly with some chipotle chilli marinade and cook for 12–15 minutes, turning and basting with more marinade halfway.

7 Check for doneness by pushing a metal skewer or sharp knife into the centre of each breast. It should come out hot. Alternatively, use a meat thermometer. An internal temperature of 65°C means it is done.

8 Just before serving, spread any remaining filling on top of the cooked chicken breasts, covering completely. Place them back into the air fryer and cook for a further 2 minutes or until the cheese is melted and oozy.

QUICK MEXICAN FLATBREAD

You can use this recipe as a base to create many different variations by adding a protein of your choice, such as lime and coriander chicken (page 34), chilli con carne (page 76), braised lamb shoulder (page 47), beef brisket (page 42) or whatever leftovers you have in your fridge.

200°C | 12–16 MINUTES

SERVES 2

- ¼ cup white bread flour
- 1 tsp baking powder
- 1 tsp salt
- ¼ cup water
- 1 Tbsp Greek yoghurt
- olive oil for rubbing
- 50g mozzarella cheese, grated
- 100g protein of choice
- garnish of choice (think fresh coriander, sour cream, tomatoes, pickled red onions and chopped chillies)

1 Mix the flour, baking powder, salt, water and yoghurt in a bowl to form a sticky dough. Divide the dough into two equal portions and roll into balls. Rest for 5 minutes.

2 Preheat the air fryer to 200°C.

3 Using a rolling pin on a well-floured surface, roll out the dough balls into rounds about 5mm thick. Depending on the size of your air fryer, you may need to divide the dough again. Rub both sides of each flatbread generously with olive oil.

4 Cook each flatbread in the air fryer for 6–8 minutes or until golden and bubbling, flipping halfway. With the flatbread still in the air-fryer basket, sprinkle over half the cheese and cover with half the protein of your choice. Place back into the air fryer and cook for a further 6 minutes or until the cheese has melted and the flatbread is slightly crispy.

5 Garnish as desired.

SAVOURY MEXICAN PIES

I love making these with shredded beef brisket.

180°C | 12–15 MINUTES

MAKES **4**

½ sheet puff pastry, defrosted
20g mozzarella cheese, grated
10g feta cheese, crumbled
100g protein of choice
1 egg, lightly beaten
guacamole for serving

1. Preheat the air fryer to 180°C.

2. Roll out the puff pastry to 2–3mm thick and cut out 4 circles about the diameter of a large orange.

3. Gently mix the mozzarella, feta and protein in a bowl until well combined.

4. On one half of each circle, place some of the filling. Fold the other half of the pastry over the filling to make a half-moon shape. Crimp the edges with a fork to seal and brush the tops with beaten egg.

5. Place the pies into the air fryer and cook for 12–15 minutes or until golden brown and piping hot on the inside – use the tip of a knife to check.

6. Serve hot with guacamole on the side.

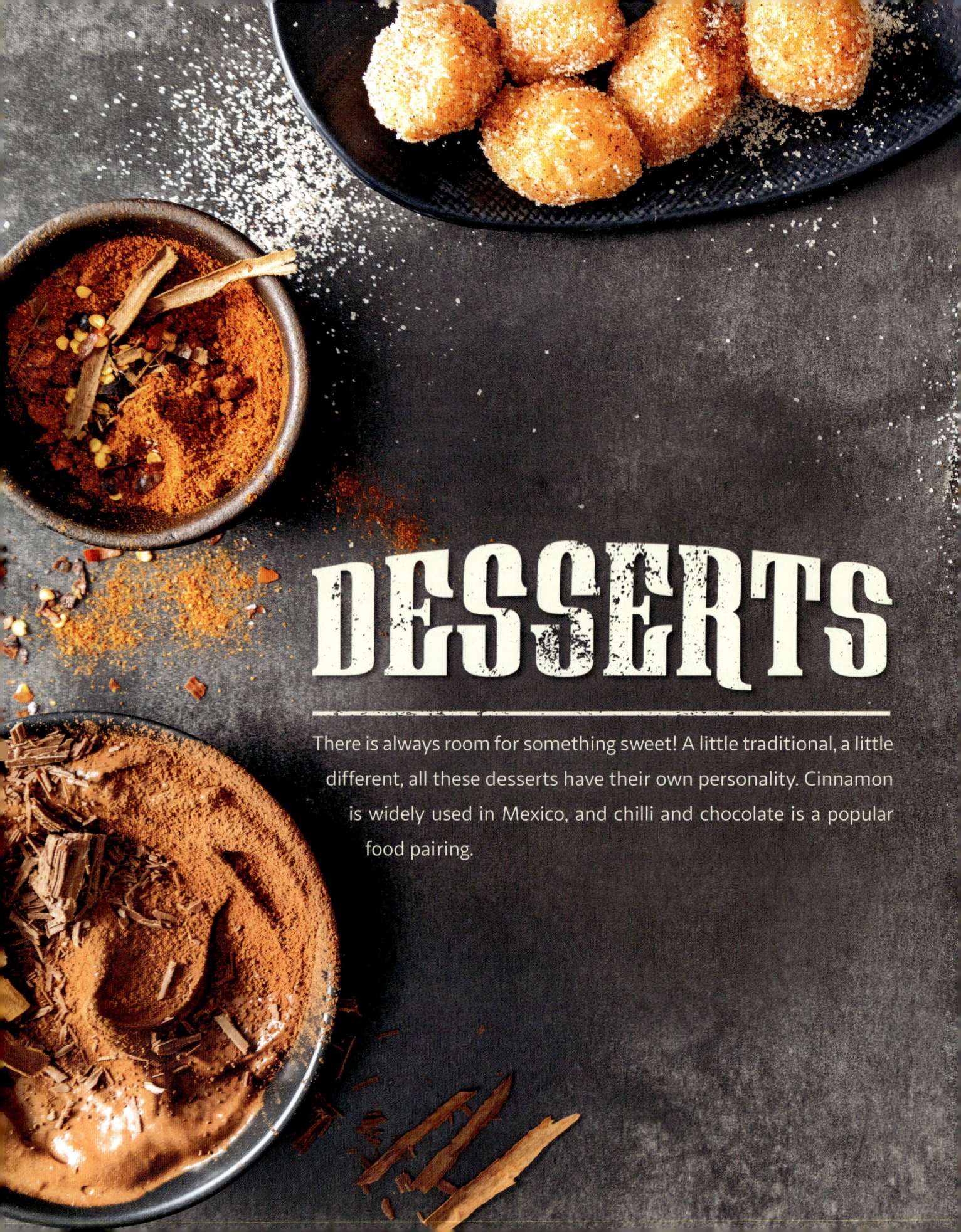

DESSERTS

There is always room for something sweet! A little traditional, a little different, all these desserts have their own personality. Cinnamon is widely used in Mexico, and chilli and chocolate is a popular food pairing.

ARROZ CON LECHE
(RICE PUDDING)

SERVES 2

¼ cup parboiled rice

2 cups milk

½ tsp ground cinnamon

100ml evaporated milk

50ml condensed milk

1 Tbsp flaked almonds, toasted

½ Tbsp sultanas

1 Place the parboiled rice in a saucepan with the milk and cinnamon and bring to the boil. Then turn down the heat and leave it to simmer for 15–20 minutes.

2 When the rice is just cooked and tender, add the evaporated milk and condensed milk and cook until the mixture thickens but is still runny. Be careful to not overcook the rice.

3 Ladle into serving bowls and garnish with the flaked almonds and sultanas.

CHURROS BITES

CHOCOLATE GANACHE SAUCE

CHURROS BITES

SERVES **4**

1 cup water or milk
84g butter
2 tsp castor sugar
¼ tsp salt
1 cup cake flour
2 large eggs
4–6 cups sunflower oil
¼ cup cinnamon sugar

1 Place the water or milk, butter, castor sugar and salt into a small pot over medium–high heat. Bring to a rolling boil.

2 When the butter is fully melted, remove the pot from the heat and immediately add all the flour and stir with a wooden spoon until no lumps remain.

3 Return the pot to a medium heat, stirring continuously, until the mixture forms a starchy dough ball around the spoon.

4 Transfer the dough to a stand mixer fitted with a K beater. Beat the dough for 2–3 minutes on low speed to cool it down. When it has stopped steaming, add the eggs one at a time, beating well between each addition.

5 Increase the speed to medium and beat for 20 seconds until the dough turns into a batter, then switch off the mixer, scrape down the sides and mix for another 20 seconds until well combined.

6 Transfer the batter to a piping bag fitted with a large star nozzle. Refrigerate if you don't plan to use it immediately, otherwise allow it to cool to room temperature. (If refrigerated, allow the batter to come up to room temperature before use. This will make it easier to pipe.)

7 Heat the sunflower oil to 190°C in a large pot over medium heat.

8 Holding the piping bag just above the oil, pipe 3cm-long nuggets of batter into the oil, using scissors to cut off each piece. Fry until golden brown – they should puff up and flip themselves, but if not, give them some help.

9 Remove the churros with a slotted spoon and roll them in the cinnamon sugar. Serve hot with a side of chocolate ganache sauce (opposite).

TIP
If you don't have a stand mixer or if you are feeling adventurous, you can do all the beating by hand with a wooden spoon.

DESSERTS

CHOCOLATE GANACHE SAUCE

MAKES 450G

250g full-fat cream

250g good-quality 70% dark chocolate, chopped

pinch of cayenne pepper (optional)

1 Bring the cream to a very light simmer in a small saucepan, then switch off the heat.

2 Add the chocolate to the hot cream and mix continuously until the chocolate has melted and the sauce is smooth and glossy.

3 Add a pinch of cayenne pepper to add a warm, comforting heat to your sauce, if you want.

TIP
The better the quality of the chocolate, the better the sauce. Don't compromise!

DESSERTS
126

'DEEP-FRIED' CHURROS ICE CREAM

Deep-frying ice cream takes it to a whole new level of deliciousness. But if you're not in the mood for all that work, you've come to the right place!

SERVES 2

250g vanilla ice cream

1–2 churros bites, cooled and chopped (page 124)

1 cup corn flakes, crushed

½ cup chocolate ganache sauce (page 125)

ground cinnamon for dusting

1 Allow the ice cream to soften slightly, just enough to make it easier to mix in the chopped churros. Mix in the churros until well dispersed and then return to the freezer.

2 After about 3 hours, scoop the ice cream into balls as big as you like. I prefer mine about 8cm in diameter. Place them on a tray and return to the freezer to set completely.

3 Meanwhile, place the crushed corn flakes onto a plate.

4 When the ice-cream balls are hard, remove from the freezer. Roll them briefly in your hands and then roll immediately in the corn flakes to coat completely.

5 Serve immediately with a spoon of chocolate ganache sauce and a dusting of cinnamon or return them to the freezer for later.

MEXICAN HOT CHOCOLATE

SERVES 1

2 cups milk

2 Tbsp unsweetened cocoa powder

2 Tbsp brown sugar

½ tsp ground cinnamon

¼ tsp vanilla extract or essence

pinch of cayenne pepper (optional)

30g bittersweet chocolate, chopped

1 Bring all the ingredients, except the chocolate, to a simmer in a small pot.

2 Add the chopped chocolate, a little at a time, stirring continuously.

3 When the chocolate is completely melted, remove the pot from the heat and pour into your favourite mug.

TIP
Garnish with toasted mini marshmallows and whipped cream or simply enjoy as is.

LAZY TRES LECHES
(MILK CAKE)

Not all of us have the time or the inclination to bake, so here's a hack to make your life simpler and easier. And the best part? It's as delicious as if you slaved away for hours. The secret is to use the best brioche you can find, preferably a day old.

SERVES **4**

650g brioche loaf

125g full-cream milk

125g evaporated milk

125g condensed milk

whipped cream spray for garnishing

icing sugar mixed with ground cinnamon for dusting

fresh berries for garnishing

1 Cut the brioche loaf into 3cm-thick slices and lay them in a single layer in a serving dish.

2 Mix all three types of milk in a small bowl until well combined, then pour over the brioche slices. Allow the milk to soak right through, forming a puddle on the bottom of the dish.

3 Spray some whipped cream on top, dust with cinnamon icing sugar and garnish with fresh berries.

TIP
If you can't find brioche, you can use a store-bought vanilla sponge cake.

MARGARITA AND CO.

What's better than one margarita? Two margaritas! But if margaritas are not your thing, don't worry, there are a few other surprises in here. Whether you're looking to cater for a Mexican fiesta or just have a casual drink, look no further. These recipes are easy to follow and super simple to make. All cocktails can be served straight up or poured over ice.

SIMPLE SYRUP

MAKES 150ML

100ml white sugar
100ml water

1 Bring the sugar and water to a simmer in a small pot over medium–high heat.

2 Once the sugar has dissolved, remove from the heat and allow to cool completely before using.

ELDERFLOWER MARGARITA

SERVES 1

1 slice lime
30ml sea salt
50ml reposado tequila
12ml elderflower liqueur
20ml simple syrup (above)
20ml lime juice
8–10 large ice cubes
1 sprig fresh thyme for garnishing
1 lime wheel for garnishing

1 Rub half the outer rim of a margarita glass with the slice of lime and dip the glass in the sea salt.

2 In a cocktail shaker, combine the tequila, elderflower liqueur, simple syrup and lime juice. Add large ice cubes and shake for about 15 seconds until the outside of the shaker gets cold and frosty.

3 Strain into the glass and garnish with the sprig of thyme and lime wheel.

CLASSIC MARGARITA

SERVES **1**

1 slice lime
30ml sea salt
50ml blanco tequila
25ml orange liqueur
25ml lime juice
8–10 large ice cubes
1 lime wheel for garnishing

1 Rub half the outer rim of a margarita glass with the slice of lime and dip the glass in the sea salt.

2 In a cocktail shaker, combine the tequila, orange liqueur and lime juice. Add large ice cubes and shake for about 15 seconds until the outside of the shaker gets cold and frosty.

3 Strain into the glass and garnish with the lime wheel.

GRAND MARGARITA

SERVES 1

1 slice lime
30ml sea salt
50ml reposado tequila
25ml Grand Marnier
25ml lime juice
8–10 large ice cubes
1 lime wheel for garnishing

1 Rub half the outer rim of a margarita glass with the slice of lime and dip the glass in the sea salt.

2 In a cocktail shaker, combine the tequila, Grand Marnier and lime juice. Add large ice cubes and shake for about 15 seconds until the outside of the shaker gets cold and frosty.

3 Strain into the glass and garnish with the lime wheel.

COCONUT AND MEZCAL MARGARITA

SERVES 1

1 slice lime
30ml desiccated coconut
50ml mezcal
50ml coconut cream
25ml simple syrup (page 134)
15ml lime juice
8–10 large ice cubes
1 lime wheel for garnishing

1 Rub half the outer rim of a margarita glass with the slice of lime and dip the glass in the desiccated coconut.

2 In a cocktail shaker, combine the mezcal, coconut cream, simple syrup and lime juice. Add large ice cubes and shake for about 15 seconds until the outside of the shaker gets cold and frosty.

3 Strain into the glass and garnish with the lime wheel.

MEZCAL MARGARITA

SERVES **1**

1 slice lime

30ml black sea salt

50ml mezcal

25ml orange liqueur

25ml lime juice

8–10 large ice cubes

1 lime wheel for garnishing

1 Rub half the outer rim of a margarita glass with the slice of lime and dip the glass in the black sea salt.

2 In a cocktail shaker, combine the mezcal, orange liqueur and lime juice. Add large ice cubes and shake for about 15 seconds until the outside of the shaker gets cold and frosty.

3 Strain into the glass and garnish with the lime wheel.

TIP
You can buy black sea salt or make you own by mixing sea salt with activated charcoal.

STRAWBERRY MARGARITA

SERVES **1**

1 slice lime
30ml sea salt
3 fresh strawberries
50ml blanco tequila
25ml orange liqueur
25ml lime juice
8–10 large ice cubes
1 lime wheel for garnishing

1 Rub half the outer rim of a margarita glass with the slice of lime and dip the glass in the sea salt.

2 Place 2 strawberries into a cocktail shaker and muddle them to break them up.

3 Add the tequila, orange liqueur and lime juice. Add large ice cubes and shake for about 15 seconds until the outside of the shaker gets cold and frosty.

4 Strain into the glass and garnish with the remaining strawberry and the lime wheel.

JALAPEÑO AND CORIANDER MARGARITA

SERVES 1

1 slice lime

30ml sea salt

3 slices fresh jalapeño chilli (slice into rings about 2mm thick)

4 fresh coriander leaves

50ml blanco tequila

25ml orange liqueur

25ml lime juice

8–10 large ice cubes

1 sprig fresh coriander for garnishing

1 lime wheel for garnishing

1 Rub half the outer rim of a margarita glass with the slice of lime and dip the glass in the sea salt.

2 Place 2 jalapeño slices and the coriander leaves into a cocktail shaker and muddle lightly to break them up.

3 Add the tequila, orange liqueur and lime juice. Add large ice cubes and shake for about 15 seconds until the outside of the shaker gets cold and frosty.

4 Strain into the glass and garnish with the remaining slice of jalapeño, the sprig of coriander and the lime wheel.

TIP
To add a smoky note to the cocktail, char the jalapeño chilli over an open flame before slicing.

MEZCAL SOUR

*Shaking without ice is called dry shaking.
It creates the meringue-like foam that is classic to a 'sour'.*

SERVES **1**

50ml mezcal

20ml lime juice

15ml simple syrup (page 134)

15ml egg white

8–10 large ice cubes

splash of Angostura bitters

1 sprig fresh rosemary for garnishing

1 In a cocktail shaker, combine the mezcal, lime juice, simple syrup and egg white. Shake without ice for 5 seconds, then add large ice cubes and shake for about 15 seconds until the outside of the shaker gets cold and frosty.

2 Strain into a tumbler, add a splash of bitters and garnish with the sprig of rosemary.

PALOMA

SERVES **1**

1 slice lime
30ml sea salt
50ml blanco tequila
25ml grapefruit juice
25ml simple syrup (page 134)
8–10 large ice cubes
200ml grapefruit tonic
grapefruit slices for garnishing

1 Rub half the outer rim of a cocktail glass with the slice of lime and dip the glass in the sea salt.

2 In a cocktail shaker, combine the tequila, grapefruit juice and simple syrup. Add large ice cubes and shake for about 15 seconds until the outside of the shaker gets cold and frosty.

3 Strain into the glass, top up with grapefruit tonic and garnish with slices of grapefruit.

SPICY MEXICAN BLOODY MARY

SERVES **1**

1 slice lime
30ml Tajín chilli spice
2 slices fresh jalapeño chilli
4 fresh coriander leaves
50ml blanco tequila
25ml lime juice
5ml Worcestershire sauce
2 dashes red Tabasco sauce
salt and ground black pepper to taste
8–10 large ice cubes
200ml tomato cocktail
1 stick celery for garnishing
1 lime wheel for garnishing
1 sprig fresh coriander for garnishing

1 Rub half the outer rim of a highball glass with the slice of lime and dip the glass in the chilli spice.

2 Place the jalapeño slices and coriander leaves into a cocktail shaker and lightly muddle to break them up.

3 Add the tequila, lime juice, Worcestershire sauce and Tabasco sauce and season with salt and black pepper. Add large ice cubes and shake for about 15 seconds until the outside of the shaker gets cold and frosty.

4 Strain into the glass, top up with tomato cocktail and garnish with the celery stick, lime wheel and sprig of coriander.

MARGARITA AND CO.

TEQUILA SUNRISE

SERVES **1**

ice cubes
50ml reposado tequila
100ml orange juice
12ml grenadine syrup
1 slice orange for garnishing
1 maraschino cherry for garnishing

1 Fill a tall glass to the top with ice. Pour in the tequila and top up with orange juice.

2 Slowly pour in the grenadine syrup – it will settle at the bottom.

3 Top up with more ice if needed and garnish with the orange slice and maraschino cherry.

CANTARITO

Have you ever seen those videos of Mexican barmen pouring between two and four bottles of tequila into large clay jugs? Well, here we go! A diminutive of the Spanish word for pitcher, cántaro, *the cantarito is a small earthenware clay jug that originated in Jalisco, the Mexican state where tequila is produced.*

SERVES **1**

50ml blanco tequila
25ml fresh orange juice
12ml fresh lemon juice
12ml fresh lime juice
pinch of salt
ice cubes
100ml grapefruit soda or grapefruit tonic
1 slice orange/lemon/lime/grapefruit for garnishing

1 If you're lucky enough to have a traditional cantarito clay cup, soak it in cold water for 10 minutes before using. Alternatively, use a tall glass or fancy mug.

2 Combine the tequila, orange juice, lemon juice, lime juice and salt in the cantarito or glass.

3 Fill with ice and top up with grapefruit soda or tonic.

4 Garnish with a slice of your preferred citrus and enjoy.

RECIPE INDEX

A
Arroz con leche 120
Asian chicken marinade 35
Asian Mexican slaw 35
Asian-style chicken tacos, Crispy 35
avocado, Deep-fried 82

B
beans, Refried black 19
Béchamel sauce 86
Beef brisket tacos 42
beef dishes *see* Red meat dishes
Beef enchiladas 66–67
beef fillet tacos, Spicy 50–51
Beef spice rub 23

Bloody Mary, Spicy Mexican 148
boca *see* Tapas and savoury snacks
boerie tacos, Sosatie and 52
Braised lamb enchiladas 68–69
Braised lamb quesadilla 62–63
Braised lamb tacos 46–47
brisket tacos, Beef 42

C
cake, Milk 130
Cantarito 152
Cashew and coriander pesto 45
cauliflower tacos, 'Roasted' 48
ceviche, Fish 90

chakalaka, Mexican 31
chicken breasts, Jalapeño-stuffed 112–113
Chicken dishes
  Chicken quesadilla 60
  Chicken tacos 34
  Crispy Asian-style chicken tacos 35
  Crispy chicken wings 100
  Jalapeño-stuffed chicken breasts 112–113
  Lime and coriander chicken nachos 98
  Mexican tostadas 105
  Savoury Mexican pies 117
  Sosatie and boerie tacos 52
Chicken quesadilla 60
Chicken tacos 34

chicken tacos, Crispy Asian-style 35
Chilli con carne 76
Chilli con carne vetkoek 97
chilli marinade, Chipotle 16
chilli mayo, Pickled 28
chilli poppers, Jalapeño 81
chillies, Pickled red 15
Chipotle chilli marinade 16
chipotle mayo, Smoky 29
Chocolate ganache sauce 125
Chocolate, Mexican hot 128
Churros bites 124
churros ice cream, 'Deep-fried' 127
citrus prawns, Peri 93
Classic margarita 136
Coconut and mezcal margarita 140
coriander margarita, Jalapeño and 143
coriander marinade, Lime and 17
coriander pesto, Cashew and 45
coriander sour cream, Pickled jalapeño and 38
Corn and miso cream 41
corn bowl, Creamy 86
corn salsa, Roasted 14
corn tacos, Prawn and 41
Corn tortillas 11
corn, Mexican-style street 109
Creamy corn bowl 86
Crispy Asian-style chicken tacos 35
Crispy calamari 85
Crispy chicken wings 100
Crispy fish tacos 38
Crispy Mexican taquitos 110
Crispy quinoa salad 94
Cucumber and tomato salsa 51

D

Deep-fried avocado 82
'Deep-fried' churros ice cream 127
dips *see* Relishes, dips, dressings and salsas
dressings *see* Relishes, dips dressings and salsas
Drinks
   Cantarito 152
   Classic margarita 136
   Coconut and mezcal margarita 140
   Elderflower margarita 134
   Grand margarita 137
   Jalapeño and coriander margarita 143
   Mexican hot chocolate 128
   Mezcal margarita 141
   Mezcal sour 145
   Paloma 147
   Spicy Mexican Bloody Mary 148
   Strawberry margarita 142
   Tequila sunrise 151
Durky Sauce, Mexican-style 26

E

Elderflower margarita 134
Enchilada sauce 64
enchiladas *see* Quesalillas and enchiladas

F

Fish and seafood dishes
   Crispy calamari 85
   Crispy fish tacos 38
   Fish ceviche 90
   Peri citrus prawns 93
   Prawn and corn tacos 41
Fish ceviche 90

flatbread, Quick Mexican 114
Fresh tomato salsa 14
fries, Mexican-style 89

G

ganache sauce, Chocolate 125
Garlic mayo 28
Grand margarita 137
Guacamole 18

H

Harissa sour cream 42

I

ice cream, 'Deep-fried' churros 127

J

Jalapeño and coriander margarita 143
jalapeño and coriander sour cream, Pickled 38
Jalapeño chilli poppers 81
Jalapeño-stuffed chicken breasts 112–113

L

lamb dishes *see* Red meat dishes

lamb enchiladas, Braised 68–69
Lamb marinade 25
lamb quesadilla, Braised 62–63
lamb tacos, Braised 46–47
Lazy tres leches (milk cake) 130
Lime and coriander marinade 17

M

margaritas *see* Drinks
Marinades, sauces and rubs
  Asian chicken marinade 35
  Béchamel sauce 86
  Beef spice rub 23
  Chipotle chilli marinade 16
  Chocolate ganache sauce 125
  Enchilada sauce 64
  Garlic mayo 28
  Lamb marinade 25
  Lime and coriander marinade 17
  Mexican-style Durky Sauce 26
  Mole negro 22
  Peanut sauce 35
  Pickled chilli mayo 28
  Romesco-style sauce 48
  Smoky chipotle mayo 29
  Spicy sesame marinade 24
Masala potato enchiladas 73
mayo, Garlic 28
mayo, Pickled chilli 28
mayo, Smoky chipotle 29
Mexican chakalaka 31
Mexican hot chocolate 128
Mexican tostadas 105
Mexican-style Durky Sauce 26
Mexican-style fries 89
Mexican-style rice 77
Mexican-style street corn 109
Mezcal margarita 141
mezcal margarita, Coconut and 140
Mezcal sour 145
Milk cake 130
Minted sour cream 47
miso cream, Corn and 41
Mole negro 22

N

nachos, Plain 98

O

onions, Pickled red 15

P

Paloma 147
Pap squares 52
Peanut sauce 35
Peri citrus prawns 93
pesto, Cashew and coriander 45
Pickled chilli mayo 28
Pickled jalapeño and coriander sour cream 38
Pickled red chillies 15
Pickled red onions 15
Pico de gallo 14
pies, Savoury Mexican 117
Plain nachos 98
pork dishes *see* Red meat dishes
pork enchiladas, Pulled 70
pork quesadilla, Pulled 58–59
pork sausage quesadilla, Smoked 57
pork tacos, Pulled 44–45
potato enchiladas, Masala 73
Prawn and corn tacos 41
Prawns, Peri citrus 93
pudding, Rice 120
Pulled pork enchiladas 70
Pulled pork quesadilla 58–59
Pulled pork tacos 44–45

Q

Quesadilla filling 56
Quesadillas and enchiladas
   Beef enchiladas 66–67
   Braised lamb enchiladas 68–69
   Braised lamb quesadilla 62–63
   Chicken quesadilla 60
   Enchilada sauce 64
   Masala potato enchiladas 73
   Pulled pork enchiladas 70
   Pulled pork quesadilla 58–59
   Quesadilla filling 56
   Smoked pork sausage quesadilla 57
Quick Mexican flatbread 114
Quinoa salad dressing 94
quinoa salad, Crispy 94

R

Red meat dishes
   Beef brisket nachos 98
   Beef brisket tacos 42
   Beef enchiladas 66–67
   Braised lamb enchiladas 68–69
   Braised lamb quesadilla 62–63
   Braised lamb shoulder nachos 98
   Braised lamb tacos 46–47
   Chilli con carne 76
   Chilli con carne nachos 98
   Chilli con carne vetkoek 97
   Crispy Mexican taquitos 110
   Mexican tostadas 105
   Pulled pork enchiladas 70
   Pulled pork quesadilla 58–59
   Pulled pork tacos 44–45
   Savoury Mexican pies 117
   Smoked pork sausage quesadilla 57
   Sosatie and boerie tacos 52
   Spicy beef fillet tacos 50–51
Refried black beans 19
Relishes, dips, dressings and salsas
   Cashew and coriander pesto 45
   Corn and miso cream 41
   Cucumber and tomato salsa 51
   Guacamole 18
   Harissa sour cream 442
   Mexican chakalaka 31

Minted sour cream 47
Pickled jalapeño and coriander sour cream 38
Pickled red chillies 15
Pickled red onions 15
Pico de gallo (Fresh tomato salsa) 14
Quinoa salad dressing 94
Roasted corn salsa 14
Roasted tomato salsa 106

Rice pudding 120
rice, Mexican-style 77
'Roasted' cauliflower tacos 48
Roasted corn salsa 14
Roasted tomato salsa 106
Romesco-style sauce 48
rubs see Marinades, sauces and rubs

S

salad, Crispy quinoa 94
salsas see Relishes, dips, dressings and salsas
sauces see Marinades, sauces and rubs
Savoury Mexican pies 117
sesame marinade, Spicy 24
Simple syrup 134
slaw, Asian Mexican 35

Smoked pork sausage quesadilla 57
Smoky chipotle mayo 29
snacks, savoury see Tapas and savoury snacks
Sosatie and boerie tacos 52
sour cream, Harissa 42
sour cream, Minted 47
sour cream, Pickled jalapeño and coriander 38
sour, Mezcal 145
spice rub, Beef 23
Spicy beef fillet tacos 50–51
Spicy Mexican Bloody Mary 148
Spicy sesame marinade 24
squares, Pap 52
Strawberry margarita 142
Sweet treats
  Arroz con leche (rice pudding) 120
  Chocolate ganache sauce 125
  Churros bites 124
  'Deep-fried' churros ice cream 127
  Lazy tres leches (milk cake) 130
  Mexican hot chocolate 128
syrup, Simple 134

T

Tacos and tortillas see also Quesadillas and enchiladas
  Beef brisket tacos 42
  Braised lamb tacos 46–47
  Chicken tacos 34
    Corn tortillas 11
  Crispy Asian-style chicken tacos 35
  Crispy fish tacos 38
  Crispy Mexican taquitos 110
  Prawn and corn tacos 41
  Pulled pork tacos 44–45
  'Roasted' cauliflower tacos 48
  Sosatie and boerie tacos 52
  Spicy beef fillet tacos 50–51
Tapas and savoury snacks
  Chilli con carne 76
  Chilli con carne vetkoek 97
  Creamy corn bowl 86
  Crispy calamari 85
  Crispy chicken wings 100
  Crispy Mexican taquitos 110
  Crispy quinoa salad 94
  Deep-fried avocado 82
  Fish ceviche 90
  Jalapeño chilli poppers 81

Mexican-style fries 89
Mexican-style rice 77
nachos with chicken or red meat 98
Peri citrus prawns 93
Plain nachos 98
Savoury Mexican pies 117
taquitos, Crispy Mexican 110
Tequila sunrise 151
tomato salsa, Cucumber and 51
tomato salsa, Fresh 14
tomato salsa, Roasted 106
tortillas *see* Tacos and tortillas
tostadas, Mexican 105
tres leches (milk cake), Lazy 130

##

Vegetarian friendly
   Arroz con leche (rice pudding) 120
   Asian Mexican slaw 35
   Béchamel sauce 86
   Cashew and coriander pesto 45
   Chipotle chilli marinade 16

Chocolate ganache sauce 125
Churros bites 124
Corn and miso cream 41
Corn tortillas 11
Creamy corn bowl 86
Crispy quinoa salad 94
Cucumber and tomato salsa 51
Deep-fried avocado 82
Enchilada sauce 64
Garlic mayo 28
Guacamole 18
Harissa sour cream 42
Jalapeño chilli poppers 81
Lazy tres leches (milk cake) 130
Lime and coriander marinade 17
Masala potato enchiladas 73
Mexican chakalaka 31
Mexican hot chocolate 128
Mexican-style fries 89
Mexican-style rice 77
Mexican-style street corn 109

Minted sour cream 47
Mole negro 22
Pap squares 52
Peanut sauce 35
Pickled chilli mayo 28
Pickled jalapeño and coriander sour cream 38
Pickled red chillies 15
Pickled red onions 15
Pico de gallo (Fresh tomato salsa) 14
Plain nachos 98
Quesadilla filling 56
Quinoa salad dressing 94
Refried black beans 19
'Roasted' cauliflower tacos 48
Roasted corn salsa 14
Roasted tomato salsa 106
Romesco-style sauce 48
Smoky chipotle mayo 29
Spicy sesame marinade 24
vetkoek, Chilli con carne 97

##

wings, Crispy chicken 100

COOKING CONVERSIONS

TEASPOONS

METRIC	IMPERIAL
2 ml	¼ tsp
2.5 ml	½ tsp
5 ml	1 tsp
10 ml	2 tsp
20 ml	4 tsp

TABLESPOONS

METRIC	IMPERIAL
15 ml	1 Tbsp
30 ml	2 Tbsp
45 ml	3 Tbsp
60 ml	4 Tbsp

CUPS

METRIC	IMPERIAL
60 ml	¼ cup
80 ml	⅓ cup
125 ml	½ cup
160 ml	⅔ cup
200 ml	¾ cup
250 ml	1 cup
375 ml	1½ cups
500 ml	2 cups
750 ml	3 cups
1 litre	4 cups